Swallowed by LIFE

*Mysteries of Death,
Resurrection and the Eternal*

Ada Brownell

Copyright © 2011 Ada B. Brownell
All rights reserved.
ISBN: 1466200936
ISBN-13: 9781466200937
Library of Congress Control Number: 2011914033
CreateSpace, North Charleston, SC
Unless otherwise indicated, Scripture quotations are from the King James Version.

Scripture quotations marked (NLT) are taken from the Holy Bible, New Living Translation, copyright © 1996, 2004, 2007 by Tyndale House Foundation. Used by permission of Tyndale House Publishers, Inc., Carol Stream, Illinois 60188. All rights reserved.

Bible quotations marked NIV are from the New International Version published by the Zondervan Corporation, The Holy Bible, New International Version®, NIV® copyright © 1973, 1978, 1984, 2011 by biblica, inc.™ used by permission. All rights reserved worldwide.

[1]Quote from Richard Champion, "Viewpoint: They are Watching Us," *The Pentecostal Evangel*, May 29, 1994, page 3, used by permission.

[1]Quotes from Rickenbacher, 1967, Prentice-Hall, Englewood Cliffs, NJ pages 243-244, were used by permission of Simon and Schuster, 1230 Avenue of the Americas, 10th Floor, New York, NY 10020

Quotes from Lynn Orr used by permission of Mrs. Lynn Orr.

Quotes in chapter six from Pastor Bobby Wilson's sermon at Praise Assembly of God Church in Pueblo, Colo., used by permission.

"While we live in these earthly bodies, we groan and sigh, but it's not that we want to die and get rid of these bodies that clothe us. Rather, we want to put on our new bodies will be swallowed up by life" (2 Corinthians 5:4 NLT).

This book is dedicated in memory of Carolyn Esther Brownell Coney, and to my husband and other four children.

Special thanks to:
Our son, Jaron, who has given help and input on this book
The publisher and editors of The Pueblo Chieftain for the years I spent there.

CONTENTS

Preface ix

1. A Mystery 1

2. Truth Sleuth 7

3. Carolyn. 21

4. What Do You See in an Egg? 31

5. Every Leaf Will Fall 51

6. Movin' On Up 61

7. Anybody in There? 71

8. Only Child's Play 83

9. A Love Message 93

10. Leave a Legacy 101

Preface

About twenty-five million U.S. citizens suffer from terminal and chronic illnesses at any given time. Fear and grief are natural responses for the patients and their families and friends.

Yet, we're all terminal. No one will get off this earth alive in his mortal state. But evidence shows we're more than a body. Just ask the person who lost a hundred pounds, someone with a transplanted heart pumping his blood, a patient who has had part of his brain removed, or the soldier with no legs. Study regenerative medicine and you'll understand the experts estimate our skin completely rebuilds itself every seven days or so, and with the exception of our neurological system, almost every single cell in our body is replaced every seven to ten years.

As a former medical reporter for a daily newspaper, in this book I reveal how science shows us that death is swallowed by life every day. I also examine the words of Jesus

Christ concerning eternal life, as well as testimony from witnesses about His death and Resurrection. In addition, I have the story from a man who was clinically dead, but revived; I interviewed medical professionals and did other research about life and death.

This book grew out of my search for everything that testifies of eternal life after we lost our thirty-one-year-old daughter to a deadly form of lymphoma. When she died, I needed to find out if I believed what I previously thought I did. Was I still certain that those who accept the Redeemer God sent and His sacrifice for sin will never die? Was I still sure heaven exists?

This book hinges on this scripture: "While we live in these earthly bodies, we groan and sigh, but it's not that we want to die and get rid of these bodies that clothe us. Rather, we want to put on our new bodies so that these dying bodies will be swallowed up by life" (2 Corinthians 5:4 NLT).

We're talking about victory over death here. The Apostle Paul also put it another way in his first book to the Corinthians:

I declare to you, brothers, that flesh and blood cannot inherit the kingdom of God, nor does the perishable inherit the imperishable. Listen, I tell you a mystery: We will not all sleep, but we will all be changed—in a flash, in the twinkling of an eye, at the last trumpet. For the trumpet will sound, the dead will be raised imperishable, and we will be changed. For the perishable must clothe itself with the imperishable, and the mortal with immortality. When the perishable has been clothed with the imperishable, and the mortal with immortality, then the saying that is written will come true: **'Death has been swallowed up in victory'** (1 Corinthians 15:50-54 NIV).

Only our Creator knows how many days we have here. I often think of the patient who was in hospice twelve years before his death, able to enjoy life and family long after diagnosis of the fatal disease.

We don't abandon our faith by looking at our eternal future. If the Lord allows me to live a century, I'll still need to be prepared for the time He calls me home.

I've discovered life is a powerful force, and all life is supernatural because our Heavenly Father created it. In this book I share the wonder of it all.

Use the question and answer sections after each chapter for review, or discussion, or to test what you have learned. If your class is a 13-week session, I suggest dividing two longer chapters and using the last day for discussion and sharing.

1. A Mystery

An old gentleman leaned on his cane and peered into the cherry-red 1923 Model T Roadster. It glistened like a new car, but just a few years earlier had rested in decay almost forgotten.

"This is just like the first car I ever had," he said, a twinkle in his eyes.

He and his son were examining four antique cars brought to a senior care center as part of the National Nursing Home Week celebration.

The man, like the Model T, was almost an antique himself.

Before the old car found redemption, from the front bumper down to the brown leather on the rumble seat, the old Ford stood waiting for one last trip—to the junkyard. Many vehicles like it have been retrieved from gullies, from behind the barn, and from buildings and junkyards, metal-consuming rust eating away at running boards, fenders, hoods, engines, and other vital parts.

Rust is the reddish-orange coating of ferric hydroxide, the substance that causes oxidation of metal in the car's body. When metal rusts, it breaks down until its elements disappear into the air and into the earth, leaving holes.

Doctors tell us oxidation occurs in the human body, too, as we age and develop diseases. We aren't eaten by rust, but oxidation causes cell damage, and that is why nutritionists recommend we consume foods rich in antioxidants, such as blueberries and green tea. In the human body, life-essential oxygen combusts and produces by-products referred to as oxygen free radicals, which cause aging.

Oxidation is part of the second law of thermodynamics, a scientific term we seldom talk about but see all the time when there is a loss of electrons in an atom. Every barn you see with the roof caved in is an example of this law, which says in simple terms that everything eventually falls apart because energy becomes less organized with time.

Our bodies do the same thing. As we age our sight grows dim, the ears less discerning of sounds. Our memory slows. Our muscles and joints don't work as well. Our skin wrinkles. Our cardiovascular system becomes clogged or diseased. Our lungs and vocal cords exhibit wear and tear. The body's defense weakens and diseases take up residence in us. Then, like an old automobile, one functioning organ goes, and then another, until the loss of a vital part is enough to kill.

Death for the human body is connected to the degradation of matter. Our mortal flesh isn't designed to last forever. Unless taken by death prematurely, like the un-restored Model T covered in rust and with an engine that won't run, the human body wears out or just quits.[1]

As I explained before, I started studying about death and life after we lost our beautiful eldest daughter, Carolyn, to cancer in 1990. A born-again Christian who could quickly tell someone else what to believe, I found my faith challenged.

When I knew Carolyn was dying, over and over I prayed, tears streaming down my face, my insides feeling ripped out, "Where are you, God?"

My guts twisted with anger and doubt. Fear choked me as I wondered if what Jesus said about eternal life was really true.

I'd heard and read what the Bible has to say. It says at death we will immediately be with the Lord (Luke 23:43, Ecclesiastes 12:6–8) and at the resurrection, in a moment, in a twinkling of an eye, our flesh will be changed into an immortal body with all-new parts that never age, get sick, or die—even if that flesh has already turned to dust.

Probably because of my experiences and what I learned on the medical beat at the newspaper, I decided to investigate if there is evidence we are more than a mere body.

I knew a journalist's assignment sometimes goes beyond the obvious. Facts aren't material objects that can be felt or seen. Through testimony and evidence, truth can be

---

1   Accidents are similar between cars and human life, too, because a human body or a car body can be destroyed because of injury.

learned. Interviewing witnesses, experts, and victims and making visits to the scene help a reporter present facts to the public.

Yet, when the story is all told, newspaper readers or television viewers react differently. Some believe what is reported; others do not. Some doubt the reliability of the reporter. Others assume the media conspires to deceive the public. A few believe the persons interviewed are liars.

Those who believe take the plunge into faith.

Doubt is what keeps many people from believing the teachings of Jesus Christ. One comfort when doubt seized me was the realization that faith is a requirement for salvation and the bottom line for believing anything you can't see, feel, or touch. The same is true for any event in history. If we weren't there, we can't be sure it happened without some measure of faith.

But did I believe Carolyn was with the Lord and I would see her again?

For months, I studied about the human body, picked physicians' and other people's minds, researched related subjects, studied the Bible, prayed and re-examined what I already knew.

If I don't think about it, who I am seems totally connected to my body. Then I realize how my life began, and I was me, even in the womb. Who I am never changed from the time I was a fertilized egg to becoming a flesh-and-bone adult.

Since I was born, I've gained more than a hundred pounds, lost some of it a few times, and I'm still me. I recall abdominal surgery years ago removed internal organs, and I'm still me. The surgeon threw away or burned my old knees when he inserted synthetic ones, and I'm still me. I could even have some of my brain surgically excised. They could cut out my heart, burn it in the hospital incinerator, and give me someone else's and I'd still be me.

It's all a marvelous mystery.

When medicine leaves no handholds to grasp as we teeter on death's precipice, we discover the Savior has gone this way before and will help. Ironically, it takes a leap—of faith.

Study Questions for Preface and Chapter One

1. You've heard people say they'd rather burn out than rust out. What is the process that occurs to the human body that is similar to rust on iron? When this process occurs in people it is called _____.

2. How many people are estimated to suffer from chronic or terminal diseases at one time in the United States?

3. Name three things you know about the human body that shows we are more than flesh and blood.

4. How many days is it believed to take for the skin to rebuild?

5. In how many years is it believed the skeleton becomes a totally new one?

6. The mystery of eternal life requires _____. Why?

7. Do you know the scripture this book is based upon and the reference for where it is found in the Bible?

8. Does death being swallowed by life make sense to you? Why or why not?

9. Does 2 Corinthians 5:4 bring joy or confusion? How? Why?

10. How does the message of this scripture compare to John 3:16? Can you think of other Bible passages with a similar message?

2. Truth Sleuth

Truth often is elusive, even when you have witnesses, testimony, and evidence. Courts wrestle with determining truth.

Societies historically tried many methods to expose a lie. In China, they used to fill a suspect's mouth with uncooked rice and he would be judged guilty if he could not easily and quickly spit the rice from his mouth. The test was based on the idea that people who are trying to avoid telling the truth don't create saliva.

Other ancient civilizations required a suspect to grab a white-hot metal rod and carry it to a certain point.[2] If the rod burned the person's hands and they didn't heal by a specific date, the person was ruled guilty and punished.

Other cruel and inaccurate methods of determining truth also were used.

More recently, truth serum, an anesthetic or hypnotic such as thiopental sodium or sodium pentothal, was believed to cause a person to speak only the truth. A similar serum was introduced in the 1920s by a Texas obstetrician, Dr. R. E. House. He believed a person under the influence of the drug scopolamine was unable to tell a lie.

Today we have the polygraph, which supporters say is 90 percent accurate, yet often in courtrooms the results can't be entered as evidence.[3]

In the days when America was a Christian nation and witnesses swore an oath with their hand on the Bible to "tell the truth and nothing but the truth, so help me God," the swearing-in meant something. There was a day when Americans feared God. They trembled at telling a lie and knew they probably would not escape being held in contempt of court for not telling the truth. Today in many states, witnesses have the option of swearing an oath or making an affirmation to tell the truth to the best of their knowledge, without mentioning God or using a Bible.

The best court cases depend on physical evidence and, hopefully, truthful eyewitnesses' testimony.

---

3 Eugene B. Block, *Lie Detectors and Their Use* (New York: David McKay Company, Inc., 1977), 12.

I decided to go to eyewitnesses' writings contained in the Bible to determine the truth about Jesus's Resurrection, which is what gives Christians the hope of eternal life. I read through the New Testament and underlined every scripture pertaining to eternal life and resurrection.

The Bible is an amazing book, written by forty different authors with varying occupations over a period of fifteen hundred years, on three continents, and in three languages. More historical manuscripts are available on the New Testament than any book of antiquity. It's difficult to doubt the divine inspiration of the Bible because the forty authors agree on hundreds of controversial subjects, although they were imperfect humans.

In contrast, the Koran was written by Mohammad, with some additions by his followers. Most scriptures of other religions were written by one man.

The Apostle Paul wrote, "How say some among you that there is no resurrection of the dead? But if there be no resurrection of the dead, then is Christ not risen: And if Christ be not risen, then is our preaching vain, and your faith is also vain" (1 Corinthians 15:12–14).

When Carolyn died, I had the advantage of having not only read and studied the Bible for years, but having taught classes from Josh McDowell's

Evidence That Demands a Verdict, a book that examines facts about the Christian faith. One significant part of McDowell's work is to determine whether the Resurrection is historical fact or a mere hoax.[4]

The author wrote, "After more than 700 hours of studying this subject, and thoroughly investigating its foundation, I have come to the conclusion that the Resurrection of Jesus Christ is one of the 'most wicked, vicious, heartless hoaxes ever foisted upon the minds of men, or it is the most fantastic fact of history.'"

When a student asked McDowell why he couldn't refute Christianity, the author answered, "For a very simple reason. I am not able to explain away an event in history--the Resurrection of Jesus Christ."

McDowell's first two books were his attempts to refute Christianity. When he couldn't, he accepted Jesus Christ as his Savior and became a Christian.[5]

I knew the Bible has several internal claims that it is the Word of God. For instance, 2 Peter 1:21 says the Bible was written by holy men of God as they were inspired by the Holy Ghost.

I'd already read the testimony of many witnesses, but I needed to read them again. I decided to look

---

4   Josh McDowell, *Evidence that Demands a Verdict, Here's Life Publishers,* (Campus Crusade for Christ, San Bernadino, Calif., 1979), Revised Edition, page 179.
5   Ibid, page 365.

again at the Bible's authenticity, at the divinity of Jesus, at His miracles, and at why we can believe He was dead but came out of the tomb alive.

Several biblical writers witnessed the dead raised to life and saw Jesus' victory over the tomb.

I noticed what John says: "That which was from the beginning, which we have seen with our eyes, which we have looked upon, and our hands have handled, of the Word of life; for the life was manifested, and we have seen it, and bear witness, and show unto you that eternal life, which was with the Father and was manifested unto us" (1 John 1:1–3).

Luke also pointed out he was an eyewitness: "Even as they delivered them unto us, which from the beginning were eyewitnesses…" (Luke 1:2).

The Apostle Peter wrote: "We have not followed cunningly devised fables, when we made known unto you the power and coming of our Lord Jesus Christ, but were eyewitnesses of His majesty" (2 Peter 1:16).

Josh McDowell points out the lives of the apostles were transformed after the Resurrection. According to scripture and biblical historians, every one of the apostles, with the exception of John, who died as a prisoner on Patmos, and Judas, who killed himself, gave their lives because they preached that Jesus rose from the dead. McDowell adds people often become martyrs because of their beliefs—but no one would give his life for something he knew was a lie. If Jesus had not risen from the dead, the disciples would have known it.

The disciples knew the earthly body of Jesus was dead and His body was changed and came out of the tomb alive forevermore. Despite being thrown in prison and threats against their lives if they didn't quit telling everyone about the Jesus rising from the dead, the disciples kept on preaching the truth so others could be saved from eternal death and live. They believed, spread the news, and died for it.

Although I knew all these things, no one was going to show me God, prove I will live forever, or take me on an advance tour of heaven. The requirement for salvation is faith, and if we could prove heaven exists, there would be no reason for faith.

Now, did I have this faith?

I knew any question about the hereafter is settled by faith. The atheist who believes there is nothing after death has only his faith—no proof. Without faith there is no answer to how we got here, why we are here, or where we are going.

I was already convinced the person who believes in reincarnation has only his faith. My study led me to conclude that men devise reincarnation to give them hope beyond the grave. People who reject Christianity often take to believing in reincarnation, which is the belief in a chain of rebirths in which each soul, through virtuous living, can rise to a higher state. People who subscribe to this belief, based in Hinduism, believe they keep coming back until they reach nirvana, the final stage, where there is emancipation for the soul. The soul then is taken from the chain of rebirths into nothingness. I couldn't understand why anyone would want to believe that because when you reach the highest plane you cease to exist. Why would I want to disappear for all eternity? And why would it happen then?

I discovered many people are attracted to belief in reincarnation because in Hinduism there is no sin against a holy God. Even though Hindus are encouraged to be peacemakers, there is no reason to repent of your sins. Reincarnation doesn't require you to change your sinful way of living if you don't want to.

My study of the Bible showed me that right after Adam and Eve sinned in the garden, God promised a Redeemer. At the moment of Adam and Eve's sin, the exact opposite of resurrection took place. Before they ate of the tree of the knowledge of good and evil, they were not mortals. One of the lies Satan told Eve was she would not die as God warned.

Yet after they sinned, suddenly the man and woman became naked, flesh-and-blood creatures who suffered from heat and cold, fatigue, pain, sickness, and, eventually, death.

In the pristine environment of the newly created earth, Adam lived to be nine hundred thirty years old. But it wasn't long after their sin that the first couple understood God's warning about what sin would do. Their guts ripped with anguish when death invaded their family and became an enemy of all humankind. Their son, Cain, murdered his brother, Abel. No pastor read comforting scriptures. No funeral director took care of arrangements. They had to dig the grave, lift Abel's body into the hole, throw dirt over him, and live with the hole in their hearts.

But Adam and Eve weren't without hope. Way back in those times, in Genesis 3:15, God promised to send someone who would redeem from sin. But it wasn't until two thousand years ago that He sent His Son for our redemption. The sins of Old Testament prophets and saints were forgiven by the blood of goats and other sacrifices only because those offerings on the altar and faith in God blotted out the sins temporarily until the Redeemer came.[6]

The scripture passage most children learn, John 3:16, sums up what happened: "For God so loved the world that he gave his only begotten son that whosoever believeth in him should not perish, but have everlasting life."

---

6 See Hebrews 11

Many of these thoughts, lessons, and God's Word comforted my grieving heart, but I continued to search and delve into everything that had to do with eternal life.

The Bible says Jesus was and is man's only hope.

God requires blood for redemption because sin is so serious. I know breaking any of the commandments hurts me or someone else. All I need to do to realize the seriousness of sin is to remember the bloody young lamb dying on an altar, or look at the cross with the Son of God's blood flowing down the wood and pooling on the ground.

I learned Jesus was God in the flesh, whom John said was there at creation (John 1:1), claimed Himself to be God, and said He existed before Abraham (John 8:58).

He also claimed to be the Resurrection and the life (John 11:25), and He demonstrated His power over death. In the city of Nain, Jesus interrupted a youth's funeral procession by touching the bier, the frame for carrying the dead. The pallbearers stopped, and Jesus said, "Young man, arise!"

The youth sat up, spoke to those around him, and went home with his widowed mother (Luke 7:11–16).

Jesus took Jarius' twelve-year-old daughter by the hand after she died, and she rose from the dead.

The raising of Lazarus from the tomb was, perhaps, the most spectacular—Lazarus had been buried four days (John 11:6–46). But all it took was Jesus's shout, "Lazarus, come forth!"

Lazarus came forth, bound hand and foot with grave clothes, with a napkin over his face.

I noticed that those who witnessed the event had to unwrap Lazarus and let him go. But when Jesus came forth from the tomb, He didn't need help. He even had power over the grave clothes!

Although I put no faith in the Shroud of Turin and would not put any spiritual significance on it if it were proved to be the burial garment of Christ, I imagine Christ's Resurrection to be such an energized event that it could leave an imprint on cloth. I would imagine the molecules and energy changing a mortal body into immortal would put off a fireworks show greater than any lightning event we've ever witnessed. But that's my imagination.

It could happen with no more outward notice than when our lives begin as a human egg, a tiny speck the human eye can barely see, but suddenly, when fertilized with sperm, bursts to life, into a beautiful baby to be born, grow, walk on the earth, die, and pass into eternity.

I began to grasp that eternal life is no more perplexing than mortal life. Our society has made sex so dirty and disgusting, we often forget the mystery and miracle of life.

In the Garden of Eden it was Adam and Eve formed at God's fingertips from the dust of the earth. Today, we know the process involves sperm and eggs, but if you think of it, the process is the same. We are nothing but dust, or soil, with the exception of the spark of life God gives.

Everything that makes up our flesh and blood comes from the ground. The sperm and egg are products of two healthy bodies, male and female, created and designed intricately for the formation of offspring.

But the sperm and egg in a sense came from the earth (with the exception of its spark of life) because all flesh exists by eating plants and meats that also arise from the ground (with the help of water, another earth commodity). The tiny fertilized egg grows from a speck to an adult simply through nourishment from products of the ground.

Even the process of birth is amazing. It is possible because the desire to procreate is urgent.

Female bodies are designed with everything necessary for the life of the fertilized egg: a plumbing system for nourishment and oxygen, fluid for protection, and everything the unborn child needs until birth.

Miraculously, the birth canal opens to accommodate the child when it is time to be born. The mother even has a food supply handy and warm.

The cry of the new infant is so irritating and demanding that parents can't neglect to feed and care for the child. But there is also a program in the minds of normal parents that gives them the urgent desire to love and nurture their offspring, as occurs in nearly all of God's creatures.

I admit eternal life boggles my mind sometimes. But ordinary life also is almost more than I can comprehend; it just seems easier to grasp because babies are born every day, and we can watch their lives unfold. But even with ultrasound, life in its earliest beginnings is almost too much to grasp.

John wrote: "In Him [Jesus, the Word] was life" (John 1:4).

Luke wrote: "In Him we live, and move, and have our being" (Acts: 17:28).

The Bible shows me Jesus is the source of eternal life. He demonstrated it by raising the dead when He walked on earth. He demonstrated it by walking out of the tomb and rising to Heaven. He demonstrates it in those whose lives were dead in sin by "resurrecting" them to new born-again lives here.

In the beginning, God breathed breath into man and he became a living soul. The Bible teaches that soul will live forever.

Quite disturbing and even more difficult to comprehend is the Word's teaching that the soul who does not accept Christ as Savior and turn from sin will suffer a form of eternal death—separation from God in an eternal hell originally prepared for the devil and his angels. But the one who accepts Jesus Christ as Savior will not only live forever, but also have eternal life of joy and peace.

"But if the spirit that raised up Jesus from the dead dwell in you, He that raised up Christ from the dead shall also quicken your mortal bodies by his spirit that dwelleth in you" (Romans 8:11).

I grasped the idea that those who are born of the spirit never will die. Jesus said: "I am the resurrection and the life: he that believeth in me, though he were dead, yet shall he live. And whosoever liveth and believeth in me shall never die" (John 11:25–26).

Yet, believing in eternal life was not all I needed to give me comfort. I wanted to know what happens to the body as well as the soul. I wanted to know more about life and death. I wanted to know if there is any physical evidence to suggest we are more than a body. I wanted to find out for myself if there is soul sleep, or if those who die in Christ are conscious. I wanted to know if we'll recognize our loved ones in heaven.

But before I tell you about that journey, I'll tell Carolyn's story.

Study Questions for Chapter Two

1. Name at least one historical method for determining truth. Would you trust any of them?

2. What is the most popular method of getting at the truth today? Do you think it's trustworthy? Why?

3. Was something lost when people quit believing in God and swearing on the Bible? What?

4. Does the Bible claim to be the source of truth? What evidence do we have for that claim?

5. Who wrote the Bible? How many authors? Were they all prophets?

6. Who wrote the Book of Mormon? The Koran?

7. Why is having more than one author significant?

8. Why do we still need faith that the Bible is true?

9. Is belief in the Bible necessary to find the truth about life beyond physical death?

10. What is it about life that most amazes you? What do you know about God that causes the most awe in you?

3. Carolyn

The music was the part that worried me.

When our daughter, Carolyn, suddenly became ill, she kept telling her husband, Michael, about the music.

As a toddler, Carolyn created songs on one of those little toy grand pianos like Schroeder plays in the comic strip *Peanuts*. She picked out "Jesus Loves Me" when she was three or four years old.

By the time she was five, she was playing her older brother's piano lessons by ear. When he slid off one end of the bench after practicing the thirty minutes I required, she slid on the other and played all the songs by ear.

Her older brother, Gary, became an excellent musician, too, but he gave up trying to compete with Carolyn on the piano.

She was eager to have piano lessons herself. By the time she was eight or nine she was accompanying Gary when he played his trumpet.

Carolyn played difficult Bach and other great composers' music when she was in the early elementary school grades. Her only restriction was her tiny hands, which couldn't reach the span for some of the more advanced music. She not only could read the music, if she heard it, she could copy it.

It was when she was nine years old we learned she had perfect pitch. Not only was she able to identify any note played on a musical instrument or sung, she could tell you the pitch of the vacuum sweeper's hum or the note that rings from a fine glass.

One time before we knew she had perfect pitch, she embarrassed us considerably when she approached the organist after a church service and informed her she was playing an E-natural where an E-flat should be. It was true!

Sometimes Carolyn would fill bottles with varying amounts of water, then show her smaller brothers and sisters how to play a tune with them.

In her early teens, she accompanied the Damascus Singers, a gospel singing group of which I was a member. Much of our music came from recorded albums instead of a book. Carolyn listened to the keyboard accompanist on gospel recordings and exactly copied what the keyboardist played.

In college, she majored in music. The hours of practicing and the hazards of roller-skating, however, set her back when she had a tendon injury to her hand.

Unless she was away at college and until she got married, our home was filled with her music—classical, jazz, and gospel.

Interestingly, she never realized what a special gift she had until she was in her mid-twenties. She didn't want to be different or noticed because of her great talent. Often when she played a piano solo in church or another performance, she'd bow her head so her long hair would cover most of her face. She also had a deadpan expression on occasion. Once she was playing a whole orchestra of music on a synthesizer with a choir production and everyone kept craning their necks to see who was playing those instruments. They couldn't even tell she was playing by the look on her face.

The flute was the instrument she played for band. She also had a wonderful soprano voice that could hit a high C with no effort, right on pitch because of her talent and wonderful ear.

After she married Michael Coney, a classmate at Bethany Bible College in Santa Cruz, California, she began playing the organ and was the organist at her church until her illness.

"She's the only white person I've ever known who could really play soul on the organ," said the church's black music minister. He had just led the youth choir in a special production and she was the accompanist.

She thought maybe the workout using her feet (yes, both feet) on the pedals might have something to do with the pain in her side. Before the tests were completed that showed she had Burkitt's lymphoma, her body began to swell from a huge tumor in her abdomen. She was taken to the hospital and when I arrived in California from where we live in Colorado, her normal weight of one hundred ten pounds had risen to about one hundred forty.

Michael told me she had been hearing beautiful music that no one else could hear.

"It's not like any music I've heard," Carolyn told Michael.

In the many nights I spent at her bedside in the hospital, sometimes she would ask me where the music was coming from.

I was expecting a miracle. I told myself I was just having hearing problems because I couldn't hear it.

In the end, there was music I could hear. On Sunday, January 28, 1990, after two months of chemotherapy that was marvelously effective at first but also had horrendous side effects, cancer cells became immune to the drugs. The cancer cells made an immense attack on her body, this time causing leukemia and spreading cancer to the liver and spleen. Pneumonia developed in her lungs.

We were gathering blood samples from our other four children to find a match for a bone marrow transplant. But that afternoon, Carolyn told Michael she felt something was going to happen right away, and she was scared.

The family that was there gathered around her bed to pray. As I began to pray, I started to quote from Psalm 34, "I will bless the Lord at all times. His praise shall continually be in my mouth. My soul shall make her boast in thee Lord: the humble shall hear thereof and be glad. O magnify the Lord with me, and let us exalt his name together. I sought the Lord and he heard me, and delivered me from all my fears."

"What's that you're saying?" Carolyn asked. "It's a song. Sing it."

We began to sing, and she sang with us. She was so ill, but her high harmony blended with ours with amazing strength.

Suddenly she stopped and began encouraging us in a loud voice. She'd never done anything like this in her life. She was always shy about public speaking. She expressed her faith and gave us words of encouragement and hope, stressing the soon return of the Lord Jesus Christ. I almost expected her to get out of bed, completely healed.

Instead, in less than twenty-four hours, she was gone. The next few hours were filled with shock and disbelief.

That night we gathered in Carolyn and Michael's living room and found what is meant when God's Word talks about peace.

The first night, the teenagers ministered to us by reading from the Bible. Our youngest daughter, Jeanette, and Carolyn's stepson, Robert, found appropriate scripture passages for our needs.

The next day as other relatives came in, my oldest brother, Dr. Virgil Nicholson, and his wife, Mildred, who both taught at Evangel University for years, shared a long list of Bible verses with us. We wrote them down and began reading them and other passages God revealed. We read several times a day those first few days.

After I went home, when I could feel my peace slipping away, I'd go read the Bible and pray awhile.

I went to sleep at night repeating the name of Jesus or quoting, "And the peace of God which passeth all understanding shall keep your hearts and minds through Christ Jesus" (Philippians 4:7).

Although I lost my mother when I was twenty-one, and other heart-wrenching deaths snatched loved ones in my husband's and my families, I knew in the pit of my stomach this would be the time when I discovered whether or not I believed what I thought I did all these years.

I don't know if there is any pain that equals the loss of a child. I do know I met mothers who lost children decades before and their eyes still filled with tears when they talked about it. I still cry sometimes myself.

Wave after wave of grief hit me in the hours, days, weeks, months, and years after Carolyn left us. At first, the impact almost knocked me off my feet, like the waves I loved to ride at Santa Cruz beach when we visited Michael and Carolyn. When I'd walk toward shore, often I'd forget to watch the waves and a big one would catch me with my back turned, nearly causing me to lose my footing. Grief had the same impact.

The first day back at work after I arrived home following the funeral, I interviewed some ladies I knew. They asked how the family was and didn't know Carolyn was gone. I regained my composure while I told them about her death and how the other children were doing. Yet, as I walked to my car, my breath came in short gasps, the pain of loss almost consuming me.

On the other hand, I found that the Lord's grace overwhelmed me periodically in a similar way. I'd be going about my business when suddenly the Lord would remind me of a scripture, or someone would minister to me, giving renewed strength and peace.

I began reading the book of Hebrews and it strengthened my faith so much I kept reading.

Oh, how sweet the Word is! To this day I'm still awed by Hebrews 2:9, "But we see Jesus, who was made a little lower than the angels for the suffering of death, crowned with glory and honor, that he by the grace of God should taste death for every man."

Jesus tasted death for my Carolyn! Jesus tasted death for me! Because of Jesus, death is no longer bitter because He took the sting (the bitterness, the unpleasantness) from death (1 Corinthians 15:55). When He walked out of the tomb alive, death's sting was left behind like the grave clothes cast aside.

I read Hebrews and continued my intense search. I was amazed to see how much of the Bible is devoted to death and eternal life.

Right in the middle of the "faith chapter" in Hebrews 11, the writer stops telling about the miraculous exploits of men and women of faith and says:

These all died in faith, not having received the promises, but having seen them from afar off, and were persuaded of them and embraced them and confessed that they were strangers and pilgrims on the earth.

For they that say such things declare plainly that they seek a country [of their own]. And truly, if they had been mindful of what country from whence they came out, they might have had opportunity to have returned. But now they desire a better country, that is, an heavenly: wherefore God is not ashamed to be called their God: for he hath prepared for them a city (Hebrews 11:13–16).

Even the book of Acts, written as a history of the church, has eternal life as its theme because the apostles' message was Jesus Christ risen from the dead. Peter's first sermon talked about what Jesus did to the process of death as he said, "Jesus of Nazareth…whom God hath raised up, having loosed the pains of death" (Acts 2:22–24).

I followed the paper trail left in the Bible, the writings of godly men and even the songs from generations before us, and saw God did something about death and gives peace to those who face it.

Sure, death means sorrow. Oh, such sorrow! Yes, we miss our loved ones, and at times we feel our heart is cut out.

Those who've never stared death in the face are terrorized by it. I'm sure nearly everyone who knows he is dying feels fear. But one thing I've discovered in interviewing many people who have come close to death, especially if they know God, is the paralyzing fear disappears when they get close to crossing over.

I remember Janelle, who received a liver transplant. Before the liver donor was found, she came close to dying more than once.

I met Janelle right after the transplant. The new liver worked marvelously, providing strength and life for her formerly dying body. She'd just been discharged from the hospital. She looked so energized and talked about how much she loved hearing snow squeak under her feet and feeling the wind blow in her face.

But she found time to add how the fear of death vanished in those times of sweet communion with God as she lay on the verge of dying.

If we believe what Jesus said to Martha, "Whosoever lives and believes in me shall never die," (John 11:26) everything about death changes.

Suddenly, some of the old songs have new meaning. I have new zest for singing: "When we all get to heaven, what a day of rejoicing that will be. When we all see Jesus, we'll sing and shout the victory!"[7]

My faith was returning. I now believed the exit from earth is only the entrance of our souls into our grand abode for eternity. But I wanted to know what happens between death and resurrection. I wanted to know what happens to the body. And I still wanted to look for scientific evidence that we are more than flesh. There were more things to investigate.

---

7   Eliza E. Hewitt, 1851-1920., Mrs. John G. Wilson, 1865-1942, Worship and Service Hymnal, Hope Publishing Co., 5707 W. Lake St., Chicago,, 1966

Study Questions for Chapter Three

1. Where do you feel the music Carolyn heard originated?

2. Would you go for a bone marrow transplant if it could save your life?

3. Is it possible to truly be delivered from fear when death is near? How?

4. Is it normal to be filled with shock and disbelief when you lose someone, or does this only happen to imperfect people?

5. Think about a time when a scripture breathed peace to your heart. Share this experience with others.

6. Would losing a loved one change your view of God? If you don't receive a miracle, is there still hope?

7. Do you understand Jesus taking the sting of death away?

8. Are you surprised to learn even heroes of the faith went through sorrow, grief, pain, and torture, while others received miracles? What was their bottom line?

9. Have you noticed how many scriptures refer to eternal life? What is your favorite?

10. Do you have a favorite song about our hope for eternity with Jesus?

4. What Do You See in an Egg?

After I retired as a reporter, I taught upper elementary children in a summer and after-school program. One day I passed around a raw chicken egg and asked them to tell me what they saw.

"Breakfast," said one.

"Slimy yuck," said another.

"Yellow...and..."

"Part of a cake."

"Or part of a cookie!"

"Trouble, if I broke it," added one sheepish boy.

I've passed around a raw egg in a couple of adult meetings, as well, and no one mentioned life.

That's what I wanted them to see.

Of course, the potential for life was destroyed when I cracked the egg, even if the egg was fertilized. But I wanted them to understand the wonderful things God put in a chicken egg. Could they imagine the drumsticks? The wishbone? Yellow scrawny feet that walk? Tiny eyes that actually see? The funny-looking red comb at the crown of the head? Feathers? The hen's cluck and the rooster's crow? All the inward parts necessary for a chicken to survive?

"It's all in there," I told the wide-eyed children as they scurried to look at the egg again. "God put life into this egg and all the DNA that blueprints what color the feathers will be, how big the chicken will grow—all sorts of wonderful things, just as he put amazing things in the egg that became you."

Life. What a mysterious gift.

We see life everywhere, but we have difficulty grasping what it is. Scientists appear to have found ways to define death; they have a little more trouble with life. Scientists can't seem to agree about when life begins.

The abortion rights and pro-life groups are at loggerheads over when life begins—whether it's when the egg is fertilized with the sperm, when the egg attaches to the uterine wall, at a certain trimester, or at birth.

I interviewed the director of an agency that dispenses morning-after pills who said a woman isn't pregnant until the fertilized egg attaches to the womb. The morning-after pill causes the woman's uterus to shed its lining, preventing a fertilized egg from attaching and living. Abortion advocates say because the egg isn't fastened to the womb, it's not an abortion.

Other developments surround life. Human pregnancy was reported from artificial insemination in 1799. In 1952, frogs were cloned from tadpole cells. In 1970, mice embryos were cloned, then other cloned animals soon followed. Sheep embryos were cloned in 1979 and cattle in 1980. An adult sheep, Dolly, was cloned in 1997.

Cloning is the process of making an identical copy of something asexually. In biology, DNA fragments, cells, or organisms are used to clone. In 1993, George Washington University researchers cloned human embryos, but there are no documented cases of a living human produced through cloning.

Test tube babies, though, are now somewhat common today. The first test tube baby, Louise Brown, was born in 1978 in Britain. A frozen embryo from test tube fertilization produced a girl named Zoe in Australia in 1984. In 1986, surrogate mother Mary Beth Whitehead, who agreed to have an embryo implanted in her uterus so that another couple could have a child, refused to relinquish the baby girl and sparked a landmark court case.

In vitro fertilization is common today for infertile couples who can afford the expensive procedure, and often the births are multiple.

All this work with living cells, yet humankind has not been able to adequately explain life or create it. We always have to start with something living, such as sperm and eggs, a seed, tissue, or a cell.

According to Stanford School of Medicine, future medical treatments probably will surround how the body creates itself out of a single cell and the mechanisms by which it renews itself throughout life. Research now focuses on regenerating sick or injured organs and tissues and the role of stem cells in cancer.[8]

One recent discovery is that liposuction leftovers can be converted to induced pluripotent stem cells, which doctors hope to reprogram to regenerate tissue. Induced pluripotent stem cells are specialized cells persuaded to revert to an embryonic state. They appear to have embryonic stem cell characteristics, but investigators are still probing the extent of the similarities.

"The idea of reprogramming a cell from your body to become anything your body needs is very exciting," said Dr. Michael Longaker, Stanford surgery professor. [9]

It's amazing how the body works. When I was earning my degree at the University of Southern Colorado (now Colorado State University at Pueblo), one of the students received considerable attention when he thought he invented the perpetual motion machine.

He knew throughout history people tried and failed to create such a machine, but the engineering student was sure he succeeded. All he thought he needed was someone to develop it.

The fellow probably didn't know it, but he lives in a fantastic perpetual motion machine as awe-inspiring as the universe, except that it needs food, air, sunshine, and perhaps, love.

---

8   Stanford School of Medicine Stem Cell Biology and Regenerative Medicine Institute, "Research," 2009,stemcell.stanford.edu/research, page 1
9   "Liposuction leftovers easily converted to IPS cells, study shows, article by Krista Conger, Stanford University Office of Communications, Sept. 7, 2009

All fleshly living systems are powered by electrical circuits in the brain. The estimated 15 billion nerve cells are neurons, and neurons do all sorts of physiological tasks as they fire electrical charges to help us live and our body systems to do the things for which God designed them. They can function independently or like a team trying to achieve a common goal.

Each nerve cell contains electrical energy which enables it to pass information from one body part to another. For instance, the output end of a neuron makes contact with the "feelers" that extend from the input end of another nerve cell. Then this cell's axon, the tail or output end, connects with the input end of another cell. A chemical change occurs in the tail of the first cell that releases a burst of energy to the second cell. The energy passes through that neuron, triggering a burst of electrical energy in the third neuron, which stimulates the next until the destination is reached.

The energy is released much like a machine gun loaded with electro-chemical bullets. The narrow, fluid-filled space between nerve cells, the synapse (actually a small canal), helps cells make contact with each other and fire. They can fire thousands of times a second.

Every time you move, think, or feel emotion, your nerve cells are firing messages to muscles, glands or other groups of neurons. [2]

The human body is estimated to have about one hundred trillion cells,[10] a living community, with each individ-

---

10   From the Bench, Salk Institute of Biological Studies, Summer 2009, page 1

ual cell having an assigned place to occupy and a specific role to play. Eventually something happens in the body, even with all those living cells, that causes it to die. Without life, every cell in the body dies and decays.

When alive, the body is strong and not only can move and change a lot of things physically, but the living mind of man can conquer, control—or show compassion and love. A body inhabited by the eternal soul can make a difference for one individual or a family or for nations and the world. But without the soul and the spark of life God gives, the body is only flesh and blood—actually, dust.

Our society doesn't talk much about our mortality and how fragile life is.

I remember doing a feature story on some fifth graders who were dissecting cows' eyes. I watched the youngsters, who were assisted by some high school students. One poke of the dissection knife punctured the cow eyeball and it deflated and fluid ran out. They divided the eyes into different parts—the cornea, lens, iris, pupil, retina, etcetera. Then the kids put the parts on a paper plate and labeled them. The teacher used the opportunity to teach about the wonders of that little dab of flesh and warned the children to be careful with pointed objects when they're playing or working or they could blind themselves or lose an eye.

Our whole body is subject to accidents, heat and cold, and a zillion diseases that can cause death.

Many of us curse our bodies because they are too fat, too thin, too freckled, or because our hair isn't the right color or we don't have enough of it. But we still love ourselves.

Kevin, a severely burned veteran of the Persian Gulf War, has barely enough flesh on his face to cover the bones. He knows he looks grotesque. The young man, in his early twenties, was handsome before his tank was hit by friendly fire. Several people lost their lives. Kevin lost his face and all his fingers.

"I'd give anything if I could get my face back, and I mean that," he said when I interviewed him for the newspaper. "I'd give my legs, my arms..."

Such a tragedy lies beyond what our minds can fathom. We love our identity, and we love our bodies, no matter how different they are.

Loving the flesh is not wrong. "No man ever yet hateth his own flesh, but nourisheth and cherisheth it," the Bible says in Ephesians 5:29.

Our flesh in that scripture is likened to the body of Christ—the church, a living spiritual organism to be cherished.

When you lose a loved one or you look at your own body and know it will soon die, you have to admit you love the earthly house where you dwell.

To think that the body decays or is cremated and actually appears to disappear from the earth is horrendous to loved ones left behind. The hands of those we love are precious. The sparkling eyes are just wonderful! The kiss on the lips or cheek is difficult to forget. To think that these marvelous things are snatched away is almost too much for the mind and heart.

The second night after Carolyn died, I remembered the tiny scar on her forehead. It was caused by a cut when she fell and hit an end table when she was about two years old. We lived ninety miles from a doctor then, and I put a Band-Aid over the cut, hoping to hold the skin together. But it separated and made a short scar about an eighth-inch wide. Since it was on her face, I always felt a stab in my heart when I saw it. She usually wore bangs, however, and few people noticed it.

But that night after she died, that tiny scar popped into my mind when I went to bed. I visualized her smile and her pretty sparkling teeth. I could see her big, beautiful brown eyes. I remembered her slim, trim figure and the confident way she carried herself before she became ill.

To think I would never again see her physical body as it had been was devastating.

I began sobbing uncontrollably and could not stop. "I know she's in heaven, but I loved her body, too!" I cried to my husband.

Not knowing what to do with me, my husband called the children to come and pray with me. I knew my husband and the other four children were working their way through their grief, too, and I could see their concern and love for me. But I couldn't stop the sobbing that wrenched through my body like I was being turned inside out.

It was so comforting to have their love and prayers. Our daughter, Gwen, finally lay her body across mine as she prayed. The convulsive weeping stopped and I began to feel the comforting presence of God.

I still yearn to see Carolyn's face in heaven, but I don't think the scar will be there. I'm beginning to look at life in flesh and blood a little differently.

Gwen now has her master's degree in nursing and teaches in a nursing school. During my research, I asked her a question that at first dumbfounded her: "Where does the twenty pounds go off your body when you lose it?"

"That's why they say 'lose' it," she laughed. "It just disappears."

"Ah, but it goes somewhere," I said.

Anyone who has studied science knows the first law of thermodynamics says matter cannot be created or destroyed.

After a little thought, Gwen told me we either excrete it as waste or exhale it when the fat is burned.

Although fat is definitely a part of someone, usually people don't grieve over it when it's lost. Instead, we rejoice when it disappears, unless a person is underweight.

Our flesh is strange in other ways because a large percentage of our body is water.

As I've mentioned before, body parts such as a gall bladder, an appendix, a tumor, limbs, or joints can be removed in surgery or accidents and we're as much alive as we ever were.

I interviewed the family of a woman who had five amputations because of a strep-A (Invasive Streptococcus A) bacterial infection, commonly called flesh-eating disease.

Both legs were amputated below the knee. An arm, a breast, and tissue from the neck to the waist were removed in the effort to save her life.

Yet, she lived a month until a virulent strain of pneumonia attacked her weakened body.

We can even be recipients of body parts such as corneas or bone from someone who is dead, or receive parts made of metal, plastic, silicone, or other products and we're the same person.

Parts of the brain can be removed and the person often continues to live and function.

But back to cells. Our body's estimated one-hundred-trillion living cells constantly die and are being replaced, which means you don't have the same body you had last year.

Scientists used to say the body totally rebuilds itself several times during a normal lifetime, *with the exception of the nervous system*, which includes the brain. But recent discoveries show some brain cells replace themselves.

Fred H. Gage, a professor in the Genetics Laboratory at Salk Institute for Biological Studies in La Jolla, California, has received recognition and numerous awards for leading a research team that showed new nerve cells can grow throughout life. A June 20, 2011 Salk news release announced some of the most recent awards for Gage's brain investigations. Gage received awards from Spain, Sweden, and was appointed president of the International Society for Stem Cell Research.

According to the report, small populations of immature nerve cells are found in the adult human brain, a process called neurogenesis. Gage is working to understand how these cells can be induced to become mature functioning nerve cells in the adult brain and spinal cord.

Gage and his team also have learned environmental enrichment and physical exercise can enhance new brain cells and they are studying the underlying cellular and molecular mechanisms that may be harnessed to repair the aged and damaged brain and spinal cord. Gage's team's scientific breakthrough was announced in a special report in the *Denver Post* by *New York Times* writer Holcomb B. Noble on October 30, 1998.

Since I had attended seminars on the human genome and wrote about some of what scientists had found, the discovery caught my eye. The report said new brain cell growth had been discovered in the hippocampus, a center of learning and memory in the brain. Brain cell growth was found in postmortem brain tissue taken in autopsies of five cancer patients at Sahlgrenska University Hospital in Sweden. Gage was research team leader.

The cancer patients participating in the study were given injections of a chemical marker to determine if tumors grew, and during the experiment the team searched for healthy cell production. Using advanced imaging, the researchers found primitive cells dividing, multiplying, and producing new mature neurons.

The mysteries of the central nervous system intrigued me. When I interviewed a neurosurgeon about how he determines brain death, my ears pricked up when he said he believes the brain is the residence of the soul. It's still a matter of faith, but something to consider.

Much is still to be learned about brain cell regeneration, but we know that throughout our lives, all over the body, as old cells die, new ones take their place.

Your body is younger than you think, declared an Aug. 2. 2005 article in the New York Times. Jonas Frisen, a stem cell biologist at the Karolinska Institute in Stockholm, Sweden, says the average age of all the cells in an adult's body may turn out to be as young as seven to ten years. Frisen invented a novel method of estimating the age of human cells and says most of the body's tissues are under constant renewal.

The cells lining the stomach are said to last five days. Red blood cells are thought to last about 120 days. An adult human liver probably is replaced cell by cell in 300 to 500 days.[11]

Researchers at Stanford School of Stem Cell biology and Regenerative Medicine Institute estimate our skin rebuilds itself every seven days, and every single cell in our skeleton is replaced every seven years.[12]

The point is the body we love so much already has died several times cell by cell if we have accumulated several decades of birthdays. Except for the nervous system, we

---

11   NY Times, Science, "Your are Younger than You Think," by Nicholas Wade, August 2, 2005,.

12   Stanford School of Medicine Stem Cell Biology and Regenerative Medicine Institute, Research article, 2009, stemcell.stanford.edu/research

are using a different body from the one in which we were born!

Nevertheless, the human body is not a simple machine. Man with all his knowledge has never created anything that compares with the flesh and bone house in which we live. Electrical circuits in your brain help you to think and make decisions. Digestion, reproduction, sight, hearing, and all the body's systems are more complicated and wonderful than anything man has invented.

When Carolyn died, I discovered it's OK to grieve for a body we loved. Life seems so connected to our bodies. That's good, because it helps us preserve ourselves when we are mortals. Yet, there are many things to consider when we think about our bodies.

One of the most difficult things about Carolyn's death occurred while Michael and I were putting away her clothes after the funeral. There among her dresses, underwear, jewelry, belts, and other clothing was a plastic bag with a large lock of her hair. Her hair had fallen out in clumps after the chemotherapy, and someone had given her a short haircut on the patches that remained. The lock in the bag was saved for matching to the wig they would get later.

Michael was going to toss the hair in the trash, but my grief was so fresh I said, "I want it."

After I'd flown back to Colorado and months later, I was putting away keepsakes from Carolyn and I came across the plastic bag with the hair. When I saw it, I felt as if I held a part of Carolyn in my hand.

Suddenly it was as if God spoke to me. The lock of hair was not Carolyn. It was not a part of her when she died. It had been cut off about three weeks before her death.

Had she been alive, the lock of hair would be nothing to her or to me.

I knew I had to discard it. The lock could become almost sacred; perhaps even a fetish to someone in the family who didn't know I had it.

I forced myself to put it in the trash, as I would have if her hair had been cut at home. Then it was as if God told me Carolyn had shed her flesh and blood just as she had her hair a few weeks earlier.

The Apostle Paul put it so beautifully in his God-inspired writing in his second letter to the Corinthians: "Though our outward man perish, yet the inward man is renewed day by day…For we know that if our earthly house of this tabernacle were dissolved, we have a building of God, an house not made with hands, eternal in the heavens" (2 Corinthians 4:16, 5:1).

Nothing demonstrates the new body we will have after death better than metamorphosis. A worm disappears from the insect scene and is bound out of sight with silken thread. The worm sheds its skin, exposing the pupa. The cells of the caterpillar are rearranged and a butterfly emerges. (Rearranging the cells of the human body could do unusual things, too, according to some reports. I've heard if the molecules of the human body were rearranged so they would not collide with but go between molecules in wood, steel, or glass, we could walk through these objects.)

Much of natural creation is waiting for nothing but water to spring it to life. This is true of millions of seeds in the soil, but strangely, it also relates to other creatures. Insect eggs, especially locusts' and grasshoppers,' do not hatch after a certain number of days or months. The cicada can be buried for as long as seven years and suddenly come to life. Other insects lie dormant, too, and when rain and vegetation appear, the bugs emerge from their eggs to enjoy a green meal. Had they hatched before, they would have nothing to eat.

When Paul wrote about death in 1 Corinthians 15, he used the same analogy Jesus did when he likened our earthly body to a seed planted in the ground.

> Someone may ask, 'How are the dead raised? With what kind of body will they come?' How foolish! What you sow does not come to life unless it dies. When you sow, you do not plant the body that will be, but just a seed, perhaps of wheat or of something else. But God gives it a body as he has determined, and to each kind of seed he gives its own body...So it will be with the resurrection of the dead. The body that is sown is perishable; it is raised imperishable; it is sown in dishonor, it is raised in glory; it is sown in weakness, it is raised in power; it is sown a natural body; it is raised a spiritual body (1 Corinthians 15:35–44 NIV).

Just as we know something good will emerge when we plant a seed, we don't have to worry about what kind of body will be resurrected.

Last summer I pulled up a young bean plant to look at what had happened to the seed. The seed was decaying, but a green sprig of life had pushed up and made a beautiful plant.

Although we will be changed when we receive our new bodies, we know we will recognize one another when we get to heaven, so there likely is some resemblance to the earthly body. "For now we see through a glass darkly, but then face to face," we find in 1 Corinthians 13:12. "Now I know in part, but then shall I know even also as I am known."

The disciples recognized Jesus, but somehow he looked different in his resurrected state.

Moses and Elijah were at the transfiguration in a form that could be recognized, probably through the Spirit (Matthew 17:3). It is interesting to note Moses and Elijah went to heaven by different routes. Moses died and was buried by God in the desert in the mountains of Moab (Deuteronomy 34), and Elijah, like Enoch, was translated. Elijah was transported to heaven in a whirlwind, riding in a chariot of fire, and he did not experience death (2 Kings 2:1–12).

I think there is some difference between the temporary body we will have if we die before Jesus returns for the church and the eternal immortal body we will have when we are resurrected from the grave or alive when Jesus comes. I believe we will be a "spirit creature" which can be recognized, but we will be different from what we will be when at the resurrection our souls and spirits are reunited with our earthly bodies and our mortal bodies change to immortality.

It's not even important, but I believe the same dust (and probably the genes that made you different from anyone else on earth) will come together to form an immortal body. The Bible says even the sea will give up its dead (Revelation 20:13).

This will happen when the spirit body unites with the changed physical body when Jesus comes back to catch away the righteous. In an explosion of power the earthly body will merge with the spiritual body and rise from the grave.

The Apostle Paul explains it in 1 Thessalonians 4:13–18:

But I would not have you to be ignorant, brethren, concerning them which are asleep, that ye sorrow not, even as others which have no hope. For if we believe that Jesus died and rose again, even so them also which sleep in Jesus will God bring with him.

For this we say unto you by the word of the Lord, that we which are alive and remain unto the coming of the Lord shall not prevent them which are asleep. For the Lord himself shall descend from

heaven with a shout, with the voice of the arch-
angel and with the trump of God: and the dead in
Christ shall rise first.

Here we have the person who has died being reunited
with the body at the grave. The passage continues, "Then
we which are alive and remain shall be caught up together
with them in the clouds to meet the Lord in the air, and
so shall we ever be with the Lord. Wherefore comfort one
another with these words."

What a glorious insight into what is to come! Yet, we
know (by faith) that the body no longer will be flesh and
blood. It will be a body that never gets sick or dies.

The change that comes also will be sudden.

In a moment, in the twinkling of an eye, at the
last trump: for the trumpet shall sound, and the
dead shall be raised incorruptible, and we shall be
changed. For this corruptible must put on incor-
ruption and this mortal must put on immortality.
So when this corruptible shall have put on incor-
ruption, and this mortal shall have put on immortality, then shall be brought to pass the saying
that is written, Death is swallowed up in victory.
(1 Corinthians 15:52–54)

I learned this event was prophesied centuries before
Christ by Isaiah, who wrote, "He will swallow up death in
victory, and the Lord God will wipe away tears from off all

faces; and the rebuke of his people shall he take away from off all the earth, for the Lord hath spoken it" (Isaiah 25:8).

I still grieve for Carolyn. She was such a gift to our family. My life is forever changed because of her life and death. We never forget our loved one, but we sorrow not as those who have no hope.

But this hope does take faith. Just as the first atheistic Russian cosmonauts to orbit the earth bragged that they didn't find God out in space, so can surgeons go through the entire body and not find the source of life. Life is much more complex than man's scientific ability today, and any philosophy about who you are, why you are here, and where you are going can only be decided by faith.

I believe life is, in essence, *the breath of God in us and His divine power generating through flesh.*

I'm confident that because I know Jesus, accept his atonement for my sin, and I've committed myself to Him, I will have eternal life and will be with my loved ones for eternity.

And I'll have a body that never dies.

50   Swallowed by LIFE

Study Questions for Chapter Four

1. Why is something as simple as a chicken's egg significant?

2. What do you know is in an egg?

3. Why do you think humankind has a hard time defining life? Do you believe life begins when sperm fertilizes an egg or when it attaches to the uterine wall? Is your belief important in this day of morning-after pills?

4. All this work with living cells, yet humankind has not been able to adequately _____ life or _____ it.

5. Scientists always have to start with _____ _____, such as sperm and eggs, a piece of a seed, tissue, or a cell.

6. Is it wrong to love our physical bodies? Why or why not?

7. Our bodies in scripture are likened to the _____, a living spiritual organism to be _____.

8. Are we born with all the brain cells we will ever have?

9. In 1 Corinthians 15, Paul used the same analogy Jesus did when he likened our earthly body to what?

10. Do we know what kind of body will be resurrected? Does this concern you?

5. Every Leaf Will Fall

Years ago I was standing at my kitchen window and noticed how a few wrinkled and dried-up leaves clung to one of the trees all winter.

One of my friends had just been diagnosed with a fatal disease. I thought how much each generation is like those leaves. A few leaves fall in spring. Others make their way to the ground in summer. When fall comes, sometimes a puff of wind causes many leaves to come loose at once. Finally, most of them are gone, but a few seem to hang on until the next year's budding begins.

I thought of the tree the day Carolyn died. We don't know why some go so early and some hang on so long. But we do know death is a part of life, and no matter how much we hate it, we all will go through it, unless Jesus Christ returns in our lifetime.

If you've lost a loved one, it won't be long until all the friends and loved ones will be departed, too. If you've been told you have an incurable disease that will kill you, quit thinking you're the only one leaving. If you take off sooner than your loved ones, rest assured they will soon follow.

James said, "You know not what shall be on the morrow. For what is your life? It is even a vapor that appeareth for a little time, and then vanisheth away (James 4:14)."

Job described it this way: "Man that is born of a woman is of few days and full of trouble. He cometh forth like a flower, and is cut down. He fleeth also as a shadow and continueth not" (Job 14:1–2).

Death passed upon all mankind when Adam sinned (Romans 5:12).

But we have the tendency when we are in sorrow to look at others as if they are immortal here on earth. I remember looking at a stewardess on the airline as I was flying out to be with Carolyn right after the illness was diagnosed. I knew Carolyn would be taking chemotherapy and losing her beautiful brown hair with the gold and red highlights. She always kept her hair brushed, sparkling clean, and styled.

I felt envious of the pretty stewardess, about Carolyn's age, who had a full head of hair. But I do not know whether the stewardess will have to face chemotherapy some day, even in the near future. I have no idea whether she will live to an old age, or whether her life will be snatched by disease or an airplane crash.

At the time, all I could think of was my daughter's mortality.

Our philosophy is that death should not come until each person has lived a full life of at least seventy years. But we have no guarantee of that many years.

close to the electrode fires, the electrode sends an electrical impulse to the EEG machine.

In brain death, no electrical activity occurs.

Body temperature also is important. Normal body temperature is essential, partly because persons with very low body temperature with other apparent signs of death have been brought back to life.

For instance, Jan Egil Refsdahl, a Norwegian fish farmer, slipped on a boat's fiberglass deck, tumbled into forty-two-degree water, and appeared to drown. But his body automatically closed the windpipe and kept water out of his lungs. His body temperature dipped to seventy-five degrees. When he was rescued, Jan was connected to a heart-lung machine, and his heart began to beat after four hours of silence.

A child, eleven-year-old Alvaro Garza Jr., was clinically dead for forty-five minutes after he was immersed in frigid water in the ice-crusted Red River near Fargo, North Dakota, but he recovered.

Drugs also might skew some of the tests, so that is considered as well.

The brain death certificate must have the date, time, and signature of the attending doctor.

The moment of brain death appears to be the time when the soul leaves the flesh. I believe it is the moment that death is swallowed by life.

As I said before, from what I understand in scripture, the soul will be with the Lord immediately and we will have some kind of spirit body, but the earthly body, laid aside and unnecessary for now while we are with God in spirit, will live again. Just as we go to sleep and know nothing for several hours, then awaken as if nothing happened, the Bible tells us when our eyes close in death—at whatever age—there will be a resurrection—an awakening—of the physical body.

I've previously mentioned the Apostle Paul's explanation of death in 1 Corinthians 15 where he likened the death of the body to a seed planted in the ground:

> Someone will say, 'How are the dead raised up? And with what body do they come?' Foolish one, what you sow is not made alive unless it dies. And what you sow, you do not sow that body that shall be, but mere grain—perhaps wheat or some other grain. But God gives it a body as He pleases, and to each seed its own body…So also is the resurrection of the dead. The body is sown in corruption, it is raised in incorruption. It is sown in dishonor, it is raised in glory. It is sown in weakness, it is raised in power. It is sown a natural body, it is raised a spiritual body. There is a natural body and there is a spiritual body.

There is so much our finite minds can't comprehend about death, the eternal, and our God. But this we know, as did Job of old: "I know that my Redeemer liveth and that he shall stand at the latter day upon the earth." He added,

"Even if worms destroy this body, yet in my flesh I shall see God" (Job 19:25–26).

But our flesh will be changed. Until then, we are mortals. Every human is at risk of death every moment he lives. That's why it's vitally important to investigate and know about eternal life. While the body decays in the ground, the eternal soul lives on.

When I think of death I'm reminded of this epitaph quoted by an evangelist at our church. It reportedly appears on a grave from the 1880s in Nantucket, Massachusetts:

Under the sod and under the trees
Lies the body of Jonathan Pease.
He is not here, there's only the pod:
Pease shelled out and went to God.

Study Questions for Chapter Five

1. Even _____ died young.

2. In the Bible our life is compared to a _____.

3. Death became the enemy of humankind when _____ sinned.

4. In 1902, life expectancy in the United States was _____ years. In 2006, it was up to age _____.

5. What three things helped cure or prevent many of the diseases that affected our ancestors?

6. Brain death is the situation where _____ _____.

7. The Bible tells us when we close our eyes in death, there will be a _____.

8. First Corinthians 15 tells us the body goes into the ground in _____ and is raised in _____.

9. Job said, "I know _____and in my flesh I shall _____.

10. But our bodies will be _____.

6. Movin' On Up

When we were kids, my brother Joe asked me one time what I'd like to die from, if I had a choice.

"A heart attack," I said, after thinking for a moment. I'd heard heart attacks happen so quickly you are dead before you know it.

"What do you want to die from?" I asked.

"Old age," Joe responded with a laugh.

Most of us have visions of dying being difficult. Those of us who have watched people's health deteriorate slowly or someone seemingly hang between life and death for days, weeks, months, or even years, know exiting earth and entering heaven sometimes is a pain-filled process.

On the other hand, I remember an Associated Press handbook I studied when I first entered the news business and wrote obituaries as part of my job as a general assignments reporter.

"Everyone dies suddenly," the handbook emphasized, warning reporters not to use "died suddenly" in an obituary. The proper term is "unexpectedly."

The thread between life and death is short, and when death occurs, it is sudden—no matter how long the person has been ill. If a person was young or appeared to be in good health and he drops dead, death is unexpected, not sudden.

We all, however, have a fear of a long painful illness before death. Some medical professionals say if a patient is in severe pain, he needs a new doctor. Pain control today goes all the way from simple aspirin and Tylenol to anesthetics administered with pumps or intravenously.

To alleviate suffering, a patient might be given radiation to shrink tumors, surgery to remove all or part of a tumor, nerve blocks, or neurosurgery, in which a nerve might be cut to stop pain. In addition, relaxation techniques may be taught, as well as biofeedback and guided imagery.

I firmly believe if there is any hope of survival, a patient should take advantage of every available reasonable treatment before going into hospice, because hospice means no longer working toward a cure. But if medical science has no hope of a cure, hospice is a good way to go.

Hospice revolves around palliative care, which means "to cloak" or to wrap care around a person. Hospice concentrates on reducing the severity of disease symptoms, keeping the patient comfortable, and alleviating suffering, maintaining personal hygiene, and generally providing all the physical, psychological, and spiritual needs of patients.

Hospice workers are trained to emphasize to their patients the enjoyment of every moment of life—grasping every minute and making it count.

It's still acceptable, even when aggressive treatment for a cure is no longer pursued, to pray for miracles. God often does miracles even when the miracle of physical healing doesn't come. When we keep our hands in His, things beyond us occur. There are miracles in the lives of family members, miracles of provision, miracles in the lives of health-care workers, miracles of peace and joy.

Living with chronic or terminal disease may be painful, but dying itself, however, is another matter, according to those who have come close to death.

Eddie Rickenbacker, the famous U.S. war hero and pilot, came close to death several times in his life and said when he felt himself slipping away he was surprised to learn it was a wonderful sensation.

One such incident occurred when Rickenbacker was critically injured in a commercial airliner crash in Atlanta, Georgia, in 1941.

"I suddenly took a turn for the worse and began to die," he wrote in his autobiography.[15] "I felt the presence of death. I knew I was going. The sensation was the same as that when I nearly bled to death following the tonsillectomy in 1917.

"You may have heard that dying is unpleasant, but don't you believe it. Dying is the sweetest, tenderest, most

---

15   Edward V. Rickenbacker, *Rickenbacker* (Englewood Cliffs, NJ: Prentice-Hall, 1967) 243–244.

sensuous sensation I have ever experienced. Death comes disguised as a sympathetic friend. All was serene; all was calm. How wonderful it would be simply to float out of this world. It is easy to die. You have to fight to live.

"I recognized the mellow sensation for what it was, death, and I fought it. I fought death mentally, pushing away the rosy sweet blandishments and actually welcoming back the pain....Time and again I felt myself slipping into that sensuous and beautiful state. How sweet it would have been simply to let go and slip off into that lovely land where there is no pain. But each time I recognized that feeling for what it was, the calling card of death, and I fought back."

Although he fought to live, which is a God-given response, he did not fear death, but saw it as a comforting experience.

Yet, even the thought of death gives most of us torment, and for other good reasons besides the process of death. Death separates us from those we love on earth. Furthermore, it's permanent.

Some of us hesitate to sign a living will, health care directive, or a "do not resuscitate" order in case we end up up in circumstances where physicians say there is no hope of recovery. We think surely death is an enemy that should be avoided at all cost, and we don't want to think about it.

My brain surgeon friend told me that much of what the family wants modern medicine to do after a person is brain dead is for themselves, not for the person in the hospital bed.

"Their loved one has already gone to his reward," he said.

Yet, I sympathize with the grieving family who won't give permission to turn off the respirator, end the stomach or intravenous feedings, or sign a paper that would deny resuscitation in the event of a heart attack. I wouldn't want to take the responsibility for it.

There are so many questions in our minds when a loved one is dying—and so few answers. We never know whether they are conscious enough to know everything that is going on. One thing is for sure, that often a person who is seriously ill is out of his head some of the time.

Carolyn didn't even remember some of the worst times when she got better after the chemotherapy.

One night she pulled a nose tube out that was pumping her stomach. I stayed in her room about thirty-six hours straight after I arrived in San Jose. I was resting in a chair, but jumped to alertness when she moved and pulled at the tubes. I called the nurse, who responded immediately. I held Carolyn's hands to keep her from taking the tube completely out.

The nurse needed help to get the tube down again, and I was the logical choice. I held Carolyn while the nurse worked and Carolyn groaned and screamed in pain at the horrible tube.

The next night, her hands were tied to the bed, but loosely, as the nurse in charge hadn't wanted to make Carolyn uncomfortable. That night, Carolyn worked a hand free and started going after the tube in her nose again and also the IV tube in her arm.

I rushed to her bed, grabbed her loose hand, and tied it firmly to the bed.

"You witch!" she exclaimed.

Her exclamation stabbed me emotionally, but I wasn't going to see her suffer with that tube having to be pushed down her nose again.

Chemotherapy and prayer brought down her fever and allowed her not to need the tubes.

She didn't remember trying to take the tubes out, and laughed and laughed when I told her about her calling me a witch. She didn't remember that part at all.

Her stepson, Robert, was quite impressed. "She doesn't even cuss when she's out of it!" he said in wonder. The night before she died, he rededicated his life to God.

We don't know how much of her other suffering she remembered, but many people tell us when the body is going through tremendous suffering, a shock system sometimes kicks in that keeps the person from the intensity of some severe physical and emotional pain for awhile.

Dave Roever, burned severely by a grenade blast in Vietnam, reported not feeling any pain from the burns at first, but then he suffered unbearable agony.[16]

So we don't know exactly what a dying person is going through. We do know from Hebrews 2 that Jesus tasted death for every man, and the taste has never been as bitter again.

---

16 Scarred, by Dave Roever, Roever Communications, Fort Worth, Texas, 1995, page 86

One person said the taste of death since Jesus is like swallowing your peas or pills whole so you don't have to taste them. Billy Graham likened death to passing only through the shadow of a truck, compared to being hit by one.[17] The psalmist David spoke of passing through the shadow of death.

Not long after we lost Carolyn, our pastor gave our congregation some words of wisdom about dying when a beautiful young woman in our church dropped dead while she sat in the jury box during a trial.

Renee worked with youth and had just received her minister's license. She was pronounced officially dead about the time our Wednesday evening church service began.

The pastor, Bobby Wilson, talked about what he learned from Ecclesiastes 7.

"We are not victims and Renee is not a casualty," he said. "Our faith doesn't just hold us up until the day we die, but it rips through the doors of death. When we accepted Jesus Christ as our Savior it was with the intent of spending eternity with him, not in Pueblo, Colorado, but up there in His home."

"The day of death is better than the day of one's birth," he said. "That's God's Word, and it's true. Our fascination with birth doesn't carry over into death. We get so excited about birth and remember our birthdays. The best day is the day we meet the Lord face-to-face. But we have

---

17   Billy Graham, *Facing Death and the Life After* (Waco, TX: Word Books, 1987), page 93

somehow delegated some glory to being born, but some horror to ending the race.

"We don't think the righteous should die, especially the young. Righteousness doesn't keep you from dying. It just gets you ready to die."

We have problems facing the reality of death, he said.

"You see, we have lived with this problem—when you are healthy, you don't die, and when the Lord's watching over you, you can't be killed. I've heard that preached. But sometimes what is preached hits reality head-on. Then we have to go back to the Book and see what the Book has to say."

The pastor said, "I think we don't have as much trouble dealing with death as we do with dying. We get into a war with death as though we have the power to curse it or push it back or take authority over it. But the scripture says no man has power to retain the spirit.

"There is something wonderful and glorious about this thing of dying that we need to grasp," he concluded.

The Holy Spirit can help us relish every moment we have left with our loved ones on earth and accept death when it is imminent. Hospice workers, pastors, and family can help with the process.

But in the end, it is just us and our Maker. If we're ready to meet Him, we'll make a grand entrance into heaven clothed with a white robe of righteousness and go to the place He prepared just for us.

Study Questions for Chapter Six

1. Everyone dies _____.

2. The thread between life and death is _____.

3. Name several methods of modern pain control.

4. Do you believe if there is hope of survival a patient should take advantage of every reasonable treatment? What are your reasons?

5. Is a person who is seeking a cure able to go into hospice?

6. What does hospice mean?

7. Is seeking a miracle of physical healing from God at odds with accepting our eternal inheritance? Why?

8. What three things does hospice care revolve around?

9. The Holy Spirit can help us _____ every moment we have left on earth, and _____ _____ when death is imminent.

10. Others can help us with the process, but in the end it is _____.

7. Anybody in There?

One day a neurosurgeon that often makes the determination of brain death sat down in the hospital lobby with me and began talking about the soul. Still clothed in the green scrubs and fabric shoe covers from a recently completed surgery, he shared that he recently lost his father.

"It was the first time I've ever come that close to death personally," he said. "I believe in an afterlife, and it was a much more peaceful experience than I had supposed. Although my father had cancer and had been sick for a long time, my dad died so quickly. One minute he was there, and the next minute he was gone. The shell where he lived was all that was left."

We went on to discuss spiritual things and how they relate to the intricacies of the brain.

"I believe the brain is the residence of the soul, and when a person is brain dead, the soul has gone on to its reward," the neurosurgeon explained.

The soul's residence can be debated. We often think the soul resides in our chest area near the heart, partly because of how the heart responds to emotion, but also because the Bible mentions so many things about the heart. A few of these are a "pure heart," "believing heart," "unrepentant heart," "imagining heart," "stubborn heart," "grieving heart," "loving heart," and "joyful heart."

Despite even many more examples, I don't believe scripture speaks of our heart as a flesh-and-blood organ, but the "heart of us." Like an apple core where the seeds are. Or a watermelon's sweet heart that has no seeds. More accurately, our heart is the center of who we are.

Many Bible scholars define the soul as the residence of our mind, will, and emotions. That certainly describes the center of who we are and gives some credence to the idea that the soul's residence is in the brain.

But where the soul resides in humans isn't important at death. The important question is where the soul goes when it leaves the body.

Many people who have come near death (some say they were dead), but were revived, claim their souls left the body and looked down into the room at their body and the people there.

My mother nearly died in the 1918 flu epidemic and told of having an out-of-body experience. She looked down at her body lying there, and she knew her brother, Bud, had died in a nearby room, although no one had told her. Bud wasn't buried immediately because Mama's parents thought she was going to die, too. They wanted to bury brother and sister at the same time, but my mother lived and her family went ahead with Bud's funeral.

The Apostle Paul might have had an out-of-body experience where he saw heaven (2 Corinthians 12:1–10). In the previous chapter, Paul gives an account of the many times he was near death, then he immediately goes into an anecdote about heaven, saying, "Whether in the body, I cannot tell; whether out of the body I cannot tell. God knoweth."

So even the Apostle Paul couldn't tell us everything about what happens at death except by the inspiration of the Holy Ghost, because his death wasn't final at that time.

After we were told Carolyn was gone (my husband and I had just returned from eating breakfast), I was in shock, but I felt she was watching our reaction from somewhere in the room. The body, I knew, was no longer where her spirit resided.

I touched her hand. I wonder now why I didn't kiss her cheek.

Her pastor was there, and he talked to us for a moment, read a scripture, and drew a sheet up over her body.

Over and over during the next year when I talked to her youth-minister husband, Michael, and shared another experience of grief, Michael would say, "Don't forget the truth. Don't allow yourself to look at it from a natural or earthly viewpoint. Keep your eyes on the truth."

The truth, I believe solidly now that I fully grasp it, is in the Bible: anyone who lives and believes in Jesus will never die. That's what Jesus said to Mary and Martha before he shouted to Lazarus, "Come forth!" and the man who had been dead three days worked his way out of the grave, bound with grave clothes (John 11:26). In another place, Jesus said He is not the God of the dead, but of the living (Luke 20:36–38). He added that all live unto Him—even those who died in Jesus whose bodies are dead!

The soul remains alive, no matter what happens to the body. Apparently it is not long after death of the body that the soul enters heaven. Jesus told the repentant thief who died beside him on the cross, "Today you will be with me in Paradise" (Luke 23:42–44).

One word of warning. Many people have told or written of near-death experiences. Some are beautiful and appear authentic, but others conflict and don't line up with the Bible.

My advice is to reject anything and everything that doesn't agree with God's Word. In fact, the Bible is all you need to understand who you are, why you are here, and where you are going.

Some folks don't believe the Bible is the compass, but I do. I figure if God went to all the trouble to create us, He would also go to the trouble to communicate with us and protect that communication so man would have that message.

Although there are many different translations, the Bible can be trusted because the message of redemption is always there. It is with other writings that people usually get into trouble.

The Bible has much to communicate about death.

We've all heard the horror stories about the grim reaper coming to take your soul, but that is not the way death is for the person who has given himself to God, repented of his sins, and accepted Jesus Christ as Savior.

Some die seeing heavenly angels, but many also report seeing Jesus, the One who promised never to leave us or forsake us.

Gwen, my nurse daughter, married a nurse, Mark Comer, and they spent many hours with the dying when they worked in critical-care units. Mark says that early on he noticed a distinct difference between how a Christian dies and the way an unbeliever dies.

I've heard that the Christian often sees a light. One lady sat up in bed and reached out to it. Some exclaim, "Jesus!"—not as the world would take His name in vain, but as a sign of recognition.

I know some psychologists say changes in the chemicals of the brain during death cause people to see a light and hallucinate. But not everyone sees a light.

Over my life I've heard many stories of dying non-Christians screaming that the flames of hell were licking at their feet. Jesus told a similar story about the wicked rich man waking up in hell immediately after death (Luke 16).

But what we're concerned about here is the death of the righteous—those who died with faith in the Lord Jesus Christ as their personal Savior. When the righteous die, they won't travel alone because He'll be their personal escort into the pearly gates!

"Yea, though I walk through the valley of the shadow of death, I shall fear no evil; for thou art with me," the psalmist wrote in Psalm 23.

In modern times, we think of a proper escort as a man in a tuxedo who whisks us away in a chauffeur-driven limousine. At death, it is the man from Galilee, now clothed with heavenly glory, but with nail prints in his hands to remind us of his everlasting love, who takes our hand and leads us on a journey to our heavenly home.

We know when the soul separates from the body, the body will return to dust, and the spirit will return unto God who gave it (Ecclesiastes 12:7). Most of us familiar with the Bible have heard a paraphrase of 2 Corinthians 5:8, which says to be absent from the body is to be present with the Lord.

The spirit will not cease to exist, or be reincarnated or become present somewhere in nature. The spirit will go to be in the presence of our loving, almighty God. He created us so He could fellowship with us. Remember how He and Adam used to walk in the garden during the cool of the day (Genesis 3:8–9)? Part of the redemption plan is that we will be with Him, and He's been preparing our place to live in His home town.

Jesus told the disciples all about it. "Let not your heart be troubled: ye believe in God, believe also in me. In my Father's house are many mansions; if it were not so, I would have told you. I go to prepare a place for you. And if I go and prepare a place for you, I will come again, and receive you unto myself; that where I am, there ye may be also" (John 14:1–4).

We have instances in the Bible that show us those in heaven are living and conscious. We've already discussed Elijah and Moses appearing on the mountain with Jesus. A great cloud of witnesses, apparently observing the righteous on earth, is talked about in Hebrews 12. Among them will be the heroes of the faith mentioned in Hebrews 11.

In an editorial he wrote shortly before he died from a malignant brain tumor, Dick Champion, who edited my articles for many years, wrote, "What do the dead know? Are they aware of what is going on in this life?

"This reminder follows the heroes of faith chapter, so the inference is that these 'witnesses' are those who have died in faith," Dick wrote. "They are watching us run the race. If these witnesses are watching, doesn't it follow that our loved ones who have died in the Lord are watching too?

"This passage doesn't give any indication that they are able to change things on earth; it merely has them watching the outcome, much like spectators at the games," Dick continued. "It is up to us who are participants to make the changes that will bring glory to Christ."[18]

Those who have died on earth not only are alive in heaven, but they are conscious, and evidently have similar senses.

Lynn Orr, a man I knew in Denver, had a near-death experience when he had a heart attack. He said one minute

---

18 ¹Richard Champion, "Viewpoint: They are Watching Us," The Pentecostal Evangel, May 29, 1994, page 3.

he lay in a hospital bed, and the next his bare feet stood on a smooth street paved with gold. In the distance, he saw a beautiful gate and a city. He smelled the gorgeous flowers, and heard singing and rejoicing. Then he was back in the bed, worrying his body wasn't covered as medical personnel zapped his heart and brought him back.

The Bible relates stories of souls with senses after the earthly body was left behind.

The rich man in hell yearned for the taste of water. The martyr, Stephen, had a vision just before he was stoned that gives us a glimpse of heaven. "But he, being full of the Holy Ghost, looked up steadfastly into heaven, and saw the glory of God and Jesus standing on the right hand of God" (Acts 7:55–56).

Elijah and Moses discussed Jesus' death with Him on the Mount of Transfiguration, so the departed person also is able to reason.

Another thing we know about the soul through scripture is if the person knew God, he is at peace.

Sometimes loved ones worry that when a person dies he will have to suffer for his sins, although he has accepted Jesus as Savior. Silly person! That's what salvation is all about. When we couldn't be good enough in ourselves, Jesus came and paid our debt of sin, and if we accept His salvation, His blood covers all of our transgressions! God the Father looks at us through the covering of Jesus's blood on our lives, making us look perfect.

That's justification—just as if we've never sinned.

I think of it as similar to a wealthy person cosigning a mortgage note for a poor man. The lender looks at the cosigner's good credit and everything is fine.

When we repent of our sins, they are cast into the deepest sea never to be remembered against us again (Micah 7:19). Listen to this declaration from Jesus: "He that heareth my word and believeth in him that sent me hath everlasting life, and shall not come into condemnation, but is passed from death unto life" (John 5:24).

Heaven has been described as a city where there is no pain or suffering. If there are tears, they will be wiped away and there will be no more crying (Revelation 21:4 and Isaiah 25:8).

When Carolyn first made her entrance into heaven, I was relieved she wouldn't suffer anymore. But it was months before I comprehended what had happened. She not only was not suffering, she was filled with joy! Over and over again we find the description of heaven as a place of peace, joy, and gladness.

But even beyond that, I began to realize that the daughter I knew, dependent on her parents through her growing up years and dependent so much on her husband after marriage, was now spiritually complete. Carolyn doesn't need us. She has reached the fulfillment we all long for. She knows things I can't comprehend, or even the most learned scholars on earth, for that matter.

Her salvation has come to fulfillment.

I believe she will be among the saints who come with Jesus Christ at the catching away of the church. We've talked before about how the redeemed who died will return with the Lord when he comes in the clouds, just as the angel told the crowd in Acts 1 He would after He ascended into heaven. The saints' bodies will be resurrected in a twinkling of an eye clothed with immortality. The righteous that are living will be caught up to meet the Lord in the air. The event is described in more detail in 1 Thessalonians 4:13–17 and 1 Corinthians 15-50–58. Jude mentions the Lord coming with ten thousand of his saints (Jude 14).

Another thing we know is that the soul is eternal. The soul will live through all eternity.

We've heard Handel's *Messiah*, which takes from Revelation, "And he shall reign forever and ever!" I notice that Revelation 22:5 says, "And they shall reign forever and ever." For some reason, He will allow us to rule and reign with Him (2 Timothy 2:11–13 and Revelation 20:5–7).

And the soul will never die.

Study Questions for Chapter Seven

1. The soul is said to have three parts. What are they?

2. What Bible character may have had an out-of-body experience?

3. We are to _____ anything that doesn't agree with God's Word.

4. The Bible tells us everything we need to know about who, why, and where. What do these questions have to do with you?

5. What does Psalm 23 tell us about how we will be escorted to heaven?

6. Part of the _____ plan is that we will be with Him, and He's been preparing our _____.

7. Who demonstrated we will be alive and conscious after death when they appeared at Jesus's transfiguration centuries after they died?

8. Hebrews 12 also speaks about a "great cloud of _____."

9. Who is one of those mentioned in the Bible who still had senses after he died?

10. If a person knows God, he will be __ _____ for eternity.

8. Only Child's Play

"Will we play basketball in heaven?" a high school student asked me in the Sunday school class I taught. "If we do, it won't be any fun because everything will be perfect. Nobody would make any mistakes."

I prayed silently for wisdom before I answered. I had never even given such an idea thought, but I said, "Keith, I don't know. But I believe heaven will be so much higher and so much better than what we have here on earth that it's like comparing being a child to becoming an adult. When you're a child, you play with dolls and toy cars. But when you are an adult you have real babies and drive a real car.

"When you're a kid, if an adult tells you that you can't play with dolls or toy cars after you get 'big,' you'll scream and howl and decide you don't want to grow up. But once you do grow up, you discard the toys, because you have a real car and a real baby.

"I think that's the way heaven will be. It will fulfill our every desire and give us so much joy that what we had here will seem like child's play."

The Bible tells us heaven will exceed earthly experiences. "Eye hath not seen, nor ear heard, neither have entered into the heart of man, the things which God hath prepared for them that love him" (1 Corinthians 2:9).

This is a paraphrase from Isaiah 64:4. But we do have some knowledge because God has revealed it to us by His Spirit, the next verse says.

If we search the scriptures, we find out a lot about heaven.

You've probably wondered exactly where it is. The Apostle Paul talked about the "third heaven." Some Jews believe God's abode was in the seventh heaven.

I believe the first heaven is where the clouds float in puffy white shapes on our air and birds fly. The second heaven is where the planets and stars are located, and the third heaven is where God is.

Five hundred people listening to Jesus teach on a montaintop watched as He began to rise and a cloud received Him out of sight. The event is recorded in Acts 1. We don't know exactly what happened when the cloud hid Him from view. Was He suddenly beamed up and immediately arrived at the right hand of the Father?

Certainly His trip wouldn't be at any speed earthlings would recognize, because a short time later, when Stephen was being stoned and had a vision of heaven, Jesus was standing at the right hand of God (Acts 7:56).

If we needed to know where heaven is, I'm sure Jesus would have told us. In John 14, when Jesus described His destination, where He also would prepare a place for us, old doubting Thomas said, "We don't know where you are going, and how can we know the way?"

Jesus answered, "Where I go you know—and you know the way."

He further explained that He is the Way, and that no one can come to the Father without going through Him.

Philip then asked Jesus to show him the Father. We humans like things we can see, feel, and touch. Have you ever felt like asking Jesus to show us God and heaven?

Jesus told Philip, in that same passage in John 14, "Have I been with you so long, and yet you don't know me, Philip? He who has seen me has seen the Father; so how can you say, 'Show us the Father?' Do you not believe that I am in the Father, and the Father in Me?"

The mystery of the trinity surfaces here, but yet one thing is clear. If you have learned to trust in Jesus, you also trust in God the Father and the Holy Spirit is involved in your life.

In this mysterious trinity, they are one: God in three persons. If you have a real relationship with Jesus, you don't need to see God the Father. You can see His works. You can attest to the validity of His Word because you've probably witnessed answers to prayer and changed lives, as well as observed how you—and the whole universe— are miraculously and wonderfully made. You know of the many prophecies that have been fulfilled.

Yet, when venturing into the unknown, our faith, like Philip's, grows weak.

Perhaps life on earth for us is similar to a young person leaving for college. The student doesn't actually need to see the money his parents promise to pay for tuition, room and board or the necessary spending money for the next few months. If the student knows his parents love him and are faithful stewards, he just accepts that his parents' promises will become reality.

The whole discussion with Philip began after Jesus told the disciples He was going away to prepare a place for them. Jesus also said He would come back to get them so that where He was, they could be, too (John 14).

The story could be compared to any number of families from foreign countries where the husband immigrated to the United States, leaving behind a wife and family, after America was discovered.

"When I get a job, a house, and enough money saved, I'll send for you," men by the thousands promised.

The wife and children often waited years before the husband had enough money to send for his family. But most wives remained faithful to the man because they knew him and he kept his word.

I think of my Jewish friend, Ruth Stein, whose parents were separated by half a world for eight years of their marriage. I wrote their story in the newspaper where I worked.

Three years after Yocheved Chalodney and Sam Dobin were married in a little village near Smolensk, Russia, Dobin immigrated to the United States. He thought his wife, child, and the baby his wife was expecting would follow soon to the land of opportunity.

Instead, by the time he had enough money to send for them, World War I was in progress.

For six years, the Russian village didn't even receive mail. War was so close that artillery fire vibrated the windows.

In the fall of 1921, the hoped-for letter from Ruth's father finally arrived, and soon the family landed in New York, ready to go to Pueblo, Colorado, to a city and a home they had never seen.

But Philip wanted more from Jesus than Mrs. Dobin required of her husband, although Philip had seen Jesus walk on water, open blind eyes, and raise the dead. Philip was the fourth disciple to leave all and follow Jesus. But at the Last Supper, Philip still hadn't grasped who Jesus was. Philip, among other disciples, forsook Jesus and fled in Gethsemane when the Master was arrested.

Philip must have eventually understood what Jesus told him about where He was going, and how he could know the way to get there. As were the other disciples (except Judas, who killed himself after he betrayed Jesus), Philip was changed by the Resurrection and Pentecost. His faith was so secure, tradition says, that Philip gave his life for his faith. Philip finally knew Jesus, he knew the Father, and there was no doubt where he was going.

Where heaven is, what it's like, and exactly what we'll do there isn't important when you're in love with Jesus. We know He'll be there, and as the Bride of Christ, we, the born-again believers who are the church, don't need to see the home He's prepared, the contentment we'll have, or what we'll do throughout eternity before we believe His promises that we'll have no more tears, and be filled with joy unspeakable.

Not long after Carolyn died, one of her friends had a vision in the middle of the day of Carolyn in heaven.

When my son-in-law, Michael, related the vision to me, I felt skepticism, although it would have felt good to believe it.

Carolyn's friend saw a city with lots of excitement where everyone was busy, as if preparing for a great event. Carolyn was sitting at one of many white grand pianos that extended as far as the woman could see. The pianists were preparing for something special that could have been the Marriage Supper of the Lamb, the great celebration that will occur in heaven, right after the Rapture, the catching away of the church.

My first reaction was, "Pianos in heaven?"

Sure, we've heard there'll be harps there. But I thought pianos were so earthly and so attached to mortals.

I assumed at first that Carolyn's friend might have seen something heavenly interpreted in earthly terms, if the vision were, indeed, from God.

But then, I thought, the vision could be exactly a picture of heaven. Many things we have here have roots in heaven, such as music.

If God made us in his own image, why would he not also allow humans to invent and learn about things that He appreciates enough to allow in heaven?

In the woman's vision, she said Carolyn was playing the piano and she peeked between the open lid and keyboard and smiled at her.

Nevertheless, I don't know for sure pianos will be in heaven.

Anyone who tells you what will be there has no proof outside of what is written in the Bible. We do know from the Word that God will wipe away all tears, there will be no sorrow or crying, no pain or death, and there will be no night there (Revelation 21:4 and Isaiah 25:7–9). There will be joy and singing. During his vision of Heaven, John saw "a great multitude, like the roar of rushing waters and loud peals of thunder, shouting, 'Hallelujah! For our Lord God Almighty reigns. Let us rejoice and be glad and give him glory! For the wedding of the Lamb has come, and his bride (the church) has made herself ready'" (Revelation 19:6–7).

We will recognize people (1 Corinthians 13:12). We will be able to eat, because there will be the Marriage Supper (Revelation 21:9). Evidently animals will be there because Jesus will return to judge the world on a white horse (Revelation 19:11). We'll have some responsibilities because we'll rule and reign with Jesus, at least during the Millennium. "Blessed and holy are those who have part in the first resurrection," is written in Revelation 20:5–7. "The second death has no power over them, but they will be priests of God and of Christ and will reign with him for a thousand years."

But heaven is still a matter of faith. Those who have had near-death experiences and say they've seen heaven, or atheistic psychologists who claim the light people see near death is caused by changes of chemicals in the brain, can never prove their point one way or the other.

We can't get to heaven without dying (unless we are living when Christ returns for the church) and until our flesh is totally dead and we're in that eternal city, we won't know everything about it.

The same human mind that can't comprehend a Heavenly Father with no beginning and no end can't seem to grasp heaven, either.

So we must accept heaven by faith.

If we want to know more about heaven, we need to become better acquainted with Jesus. If we know the heavenly bridegroom, and believe that He's preparing a place for us, that's all we need to know.

Study Questions for Chapter Eight

1. Heaven probably can be compared to the difference between being a _____ and becoming an _____.

2. Heaven will _____earthly experiences.

3. Has God revealed anything about what is in store for us?

4. Is there more than one place termed "heaven?" Explain.

5. How do we know that when gravity let loose of Jesus and He went up in a cloud that He quickly arrived in heaven?

6. Do we know exactly where heaven is located?

7. Do you know how to get there? How do we get there?

8. Do you sometimes feel like Philip, who wanted to see God the Father with his own eyes? Why? Do you feel you know God the Father and God the Son?

9. Why don't we need to see the Father?

10. Where heaven is, what it's like, and exactly what we'll do there isn't important when _____ .

9. A Love Message

One time as we were traveling, I was in the back seat resting with my eyes closed and began thinking about how Carolyn's young life was cut short.

Previously when grief hit me, I'd often catch my breath and begin whispering the name of Jesus. This day, however, tears oozed through my eyelids.

"Lord, heaven is so silent!" I complained.

I had prayed for months, grasping onto God in faith, continually staying in the Word and prayer. Most of the time, peace filled me. That day, a poisonous bitterness erupted instead as I complained about feeling forsaken.

Then, I felt rebuke.

It wasn't an audible voice, but in my spirit I could hear Jesus tell me, "I made a statement about my love for you two thousand years ago on the cross that still echoes around the world. That is enough."

Just as quickly as I felt anger, which is one of the stages of grief, I felt overwhelmed with God's love for me. Yes! The cross was enough. It not only was enough to show God's love for me and my daughter, but it also gave anyone who will accept His love hope because death will be swallowed by life for all eternity.

No wonder people can face death with peace. No wonder there is joy, even when we know life on earth is temporary. No wonder sin holds no attraction for many! No wonder people rejoice that while we were yet sinners, Christ died for the ungodly (Romans 5:6–8).

Many people have an erroneous view of God.

One time my coworkers were in a discussion in which I didn't participate because I was busy at my desk. Then one of those entrenched in the debate paused long enough to ask me, "Isn't that right, Ada? God carries a big stick."

"I don't know how you can say that and look at the cross," I responded.

If you want to know about God, read the Bible for yourself. Beginning with Genesis and ending with Revelation, it is a story about redemption—for you. Redemption from sins, which means when you repent they're wiped out—erased from the record (Micah 7:17-19). Redemption from Satan, who would like to have you (Luke 22:31). Redemption from the eternal death sentence on your head (John 5:23-25).

"For it is appointed unto man once to die, but after this the judgment. So Christ was offered once to bear the sins of many. To those who eagerly wait for Him, He will appear the second time, without sin, for salvation" (Hebrews 9:27).

To get an idea of salvation in a nutshell, start with John's Gospel.

Hearing the Word, reading the Word, and keeping a prayer on our lips is how we get to know God better. We can talk to God when we're angry with Him or people around us. We can talk to God when all we can think of is, "Why?"

When grief hits us like a huge wave of the sea, we can get up and purpose to know God better. Through our trials, we learn God is faithful. In our struggling and in our weakness, suddenly we understand we can ride grief's thunderous waters instead of letting them knock us off our feet.

We find that God's grace and love come like waves, too, lifting us up with joy as we learn that He created us for eternal life in the beginning, and the miracle still happens. Death is swallowed by life.

Those who have gone before us show there is hope, even in death.

I think of the many martyrs who have died for their faith. During the Russian Revolution many Christians gave their lives for the Lord, knowing that hope goes beyond this life.

"We divided into groups of ten," said one Russian pastor. "In case one is shot or imprisoned, the next in rank steps into line. One of our pastors who stood for Christ in a Communistic gathering was watched and followed by the secret police. While he was preaching in his own pulpit, they entered and arrested him. Later, our congregation received a note saying, 'If you wish to find the body of your pastor, go to a certain cemetery.'

"We found him shot dead with his Bible on his breast. They had offered him a large reward if he would renounce Christ, but he chose death with Christ."[19]

To have this supernatural peace, we must know Jesus. We must accept Him as our Savior—the reason He came to this world.

Many people believe having some good qualities during our life means we'll go to heaven.

If we could be good enough in ourselves, Jesus wouldn't have given up His throne in heaven to come to earth and suffer a humiliating and painful death on the cross. Because He knew we couldn't get to Heaven without His sacrifice, He gave His back to the a cat-o'-nine-tails, allowed spikes to be driven through His hands and feet, the crown of thorns jammed on His head, His beard plucked, His clothing ripped off. He endured the agony of gravity pulling at the nails, and allowed the spear to pierce His side. All of this suffering fulfilled prophesies written centuries before.

Don't ever forget there was a reason Jesus died there, his nearly naked body stretched above the earth for all to see. A blood sacrifice was needed to atone for sin because

---

19   James and Marti Hefley, By Their Blood: Christian Martyrs of the 20th Century (Milford, MI: Mott Media, 1979), page 241

sin is so terrible. Look at the Ten Commandments. Breaking any of them hurts either you or someone else.

He chose to die—so that we could have eternal life. And God the Father chose to send His Son, not only because He loved us, but because He promised a redeemer right after Adam and Eve sinned in the Garden of Eden (Genesis 3:15).

The Apostle Paul told Titus we don't become righteous because of works we have done, but by His mercy God saves us from sin and eternal death (Titus 3:5).

It's up to us what we do about redemption.

Perhaps you don't trust the Bible. What more reliable source do you have?

I believe if God loves man enough, as He said He does, He would make sure the Bible was preserved with the message He intended man to hear.

Never in all of history has any writing been preserved with more diligence. It is the most reliable book of antiquity because compared to other ancient writings, the Bible has more manuscript evidence to support it than any ten pieces of classical literature combined.[20] Scribes copied the Old Testament and did nothing else. Their work had such a devotion to accuracy that every consonant and vowel was checked and rechecked.

Archaeology has confirmed that people mentioned in the Bible lived, cities mentioned there existed, and historical facts jibe with other historical writings.

---

20   Josh McDowell, The New Evidence that Demands a Verdict, 1999, Here's Life Publishers, page 9

Not everything in the Bible has been confirmed, however, by science or history, partly because it takes so long to sift through buried empires and because some scientists' opinions are prejudiced against the Bible.

But the Bible is not a book of history; it is a book of redemption. The story begins with man's conviction to death, and ends with humans transformed to immortal creatures drinking from the River of Life.

Each of us needs to accept Christ, and if you haven't, you should do so immediately.

The Bible says, "Now is the day of Salvation" (2 Corinthians 6:2).

The Bible says we first must believe in Him, then repent by confessing our sins to Him, then telling others or showing others that we are followers of Christ. "If we confess our sins, He is faithful and just to forgive us our sins and to cleanse us from all unrighteousness. For with the heart one believes unto righteousness and with the mouth confession is made unto salvation" (Romans 10:9–10).

All sorts of benefits, such as joy, comfort and peace, come with salvation.

When Jesus talked about returning to Heaven, He told His disciples the Holy Spirit would come. "I will pray the Father and He will give you another Comforter, that He may abide with you forever, even the Spirit of truth, whom the world can't receive because it neither sees Him nor knows Him; but you know Him, for He dwells with you and will be in you.

"I will not leave you comfortless. I will come to you. A little while longer and the world will see me no more, but you will see me. Because I live, you will live also" (John 14:16–19).

That's death swallowed by life, and there is great comfort in knowing that!

Study Questions for Chapter Nine

1. Is it normal for people who are grieving to feel anger?

2. Can people sometimes feel rebuke from the Lord when their thoughts and attitude remain stuck in anger? Why?

3. Why does the Lord sometimes stop speaking comfort to us when we dwell on our grief and don't move forward in faith?

4. Is Jesus's declaration of love for you when He laid down His life on the cross enough to comfort you? Why?

5. His death gave anyone who will accept His love hope that death will be _____ by _____ for all eternity.

6. No wonder there is joy, even when we know life on earth is _____.

7. Hebrews 9:27 tells us "It is appointed unto man _____ to _____, but after this, the _____.

8. "So Christ was offered once to bear the ____ of many. To those who eagerly wait for Him, He will _____, without sin, for salvation."

9. _____ the Word, _____ the Word, and keeping a _____ on our lips is how we get to know God better. We can talk to God when all we can think of is _____.

10. He created us for _____ _____ in the beginning, and the miracle still happens. Death is _____ by life.

10. Leave a Legacy

Two signers of the Declaration of Independence in their last wills and testaments left testimonies to their families and urged them to follow Christ: Patrick Henry and Richard Stockton.

Our generation hasn't given much attention to the "testament" part you leave along with your worldly goods. Some attorneys today would argue that a will and a testament are the same. The dictionary, however, describes testament as "a covenant, particularly between God and man." A testimony is "an affirmation of beliefs or convictions."

In times past, many people left testaments for their families.

One person who did this was a woman who was diagnosed with terminal cancer in the days before treatments gave more hope.

"If you think about it," she wrote, "knowing when you are going to die has its advantages. That way before you go, you can tie your life up with a beautiful bow."

She spoke of choosing who you would like to receive your treasured possessions.

An attorney gave us a form to fill with a list of things to be given to certain people—small things like teapots, the huge painting of Great-Grandma, the china, the coin collection, and the silver. Never mind we don't have any of these things. But we do have some possessions that members of our family might cherish. If more people made these detailed wills, there probably would be less feuding among family members when a loved one passes away.

But not leaving loose ends goes beyond writing a detailed will—it helps the family to know you better.

Hospice workers tell us many family members often avoid talking to a patient about inevitable death. They also tell us it helps to ensure a peaceful death if each family member comes to grips with the shortness of time and takes the opportunity to mend broken relationships and heal hurts and misunderstandings. The patient who forgives and loves even the unlovable finds peace and joy as he faces the future, and it helps those left behind tremendously.

Conversations aren't as permanent as things recorded electronically or written, however. It's the testament that will remain when the inherited money is spent, the house is in disrepair, the jewelry lost or stolen, the china broken, the furniture scarred and out of style, and many important things said forgotten.

Our Carolyn left us a prayer letter she wrote about a year before she passed away. She didn't know she was leaving us because she died only two months after the lymphoma diagnosis. But she wrote a letter thanking us for the way she was raised, mentioning specific things we taught her that she considered valuable. Then she wrote short prayers for each member of our immediate family. These documents are priceless.

I have a wonderful salvation testimony on cassette tape from one of my aunts that's also priceless. She gave the testimony when she spoke for a women's group, but it became a testament after her death at age ninety-five. I probably need to transfer the cassette to a CD or the latest electronic recording device.

We have a tape of my grandmother, an orator in her day, reciting the poem for which she was most known: a humorous sermon-type variation on the nursery rhyme "Old Mother Hubbard." We have recordings of Grandma playing the piano and singing with her high-pitched, right-on-key vocals that filled a room similar to xylophone notes flowing around our heads like bubbles. We remember her commitment to God, as well, many decades after her death. In a way, all these things are part of her testament.

My grandfather left a testament of sorts to his children because he frequently sang the old hymn "The Ninety and Nine." The words relate how Jesus said if He has one lost sheep He will leave ninety-nine and seek to save the missing one. Grandpa's children could almost hear him singing the song until death also took them home.

My mother died unexpectedly from a stroke at age fifty-eight, yet she left a legacy of scrapbooks about her beliefs, such as the perils of liquor and the importance of serving God. The spiritual training she gave us also is a legacy that still makes a difference in our lives.

I and my brothers and sisters, especially we red-headed ones, still can hear her quoting the scripture, "Let every man be swift to hear, slow to speak and slow to wrath" (James 1:19). These things are testaments, too.

Yet, formal testaments drawn up and designed as a legacy for loved ones go farther.

When you write or record a testament, tell your family why you are the person you are. You can pick and choose what you want to include and choose the people to whom you want to give a testament. You can leave one general testament for everyone, or prepare one for each of the special people in your life. These can be read or played after you are gone.

Here are suggestions for things to include. It will be much better if you use detail, paint the scenes with words, using the senses.

- If you are a Christian, tell what brought you to accept the Lord Jesus Christ as your Savior, why you did it, and how God impacted your life.
- Favorite memories of loved ones and friends.
- The funniest thing that happened to you.
- Miracles and significant answers to prayer.
- Things for which you thank God.

- Things for which you thank loved ones. You can be specific if you desire, but be sure you don't leave anyone out.
- Times when God amazed you. You might relate miracles that you have witnessed or were told about by reliable witnesses.
- Why you love God.
- Why you love the person to whom the letter is addressed.
- A prayer for each of your loved ones.
- A promise to meet each person in heaven and how important it is to you that they be with you for eternity.

Tell your family and loved ones (if they don't know or aren't ready) how they can inherit eternal life so you will meet again.

Use scriptures such as these.
- Romans 3:23: "For all have sinned and come short of the glory of God."
- John 3:16: "For God so loved the world that he gave his only begotten son, that whosoever believeth in him should not perish but have eternal life."
- 1 John 1:9: "If we confess our sins, he is faithful and just to forgive us our sins and to cleanse us from all unrighteousness."
- Romans 10:9: "If thou shalt confess with thy mouth the Lord Jesus and believe in thy heart that God has raised him from the dead, thou shalt be saved."

- Matthew 16:23–25: "If anyone desires to come after me, let him deny himself, and take up his cross, and follow me."
- James 1:12: "Blessed is the man that endureth temptation: for when he is tried, he shall receive the crown of life, which the Lord hath promised to them that love him."

Let your loved ones know that when the roll is read in heaven, when time is no more, you'll be listening for their names to be called from the Book of Life and you're planning a reunion in the New Jerusalem. Because death has been swallowed by life!

Study Questions for Chapter Ten

1. What is a testament?

2. Is it important to leave a will and testament even if you don't have many worldly goods? Why?

3. If more people made detailed wills, there probably would be less _____ among family members when a loved one passes away.

4. Hospice workers tell us many family members often _____ talking to a patient about _____.

5. They also tell us it helps to ensure a peaceful death if each family member takes the opportunity to _____ _____.

6. When you write or record a testament, tell your family why you are _____and _____.

7. What are some other things you can put in your testament?

8. Has someone in your family given you something in a will or testament that you value? Why do you value it?

9. What would you like most to leave behind for your loved ones?

10. How would you like to be remembered?

Answers to Study Questions

Chapter One

1. Oxidation. Aging.
2. Twenty-five million
3. We start as a tiny egg. Organs and other body parts can be removed or transplanted from another person and it doesn't change who the person is. Cell death and regeneration. Weight gain and loss.
4. Seven days.
5. Seven years.
6. A leap of faith. Because there is no way we can prove it exists beyond the grave and because faith is required for Salvation—the way to eternal life.
7. "While we live in these earthly bodies, we groan and sigh, but it's not that we want to die and get rid of these bodies that clothe us. Rather, we want to put on our new bodies so that these dying bodies will be swallowed up by life" (2 Corinthians 5:4 NLT).
8. Answers here depend on each individual. Be truthful to yourself.
9. Same as above.
10. Same as above.

Chapter Two

1. The polygraph lie detector, rice in the mouth, making a person grasp a hot rod, truth serum.

2. The polygraph. It's not admissible in most courts as evidence. Truth often is elusive.
3. Believing in God and keeping the commandment, "Thou shalt not bear false witness" causes people to tell the truth as nothing else can. When that is lost, whose word can you trust?
4. Yes. There are numerous references, including 2 Peter 1:21 and John 17:16–18.
5. Forty different authors with varying occupations, inspired by the Holy Ghost over a period of one thousand five hundred years, on three continents, and in three languages.
6. Joseph Smith. Mohammad, with some additions by his followers.
7. Because they all agree on hundreds of controversial subjects, although they were imperfect humans.
8. Because faith is necessary for salvation.
9. Jesus is the only way of salvation and the Bible reveals Him to us. At least a person needs to hear what's written in the Bible, the story of redemption, to believe and receive salvation.
10. Think about what you believe, then share your thoughts.

Chapter Three

1. The author believes the music was heavenly, but give your own answer.
2. Again, give your own opinion.

110 **Swallowed by LIFE**

3. Through faith and God's grace and mercy.
4. These feelings are normal stages of grief.
5. Share your thoughts.
6. Losing someone to death helps us find out whether we believe what we think we do. 1 Corinthians 13 says hope abides forever.
7. 1 Corinthians 15:56 says, "The sting of death is sin," and if we have repented of our sins and accepted Jesus as Savior, sin and the sting are gone. The previous verse says, "Death is swallowed up in victory. O death, where is your sting?"
8. They were seeking another country, eternal in the heavens, whose Builder and Maker is God (Hebrews 11).
9. Share your favorite scriptures about eternal life.
10. Hymnbooks are full of songs about heaven. One of the author's favorites is "The Unclouded Day."

Chapter Four

1. Because God saw us and loved us when we were just an egg in our mother's womb, but also to show what an amazing God we have who can put all the miraculous systems into a bunch of slime.
2. Life, if fertilized—all the DNA and inward parts needed to make the newborn like his ancestors, but also a unique design made by God. Also included are the seeing eyes, the hearing ears, the voice, and all the wonder created in us all.

3. We have trouble defining life because the mystery of it is beyond comprehension without acknowledging God. Admitting the truth of when life begins with the fertilized egg helps us understand that a morning-after pill after the sperm has connected with the egg actually is an abortion.
4. Explain life or create it.
5. Something living.
6. Loving the flesh is not wrong. "No man ever yet hateth his own flesh, but nourisheth and cherisheth it," the Bible says in Ephesians 5:29.
7. The church, cherished.
8. No. Gage's studies show neurons (brain cells) constantly are being born, particularly in learning and memory centers. The source of the new cells is neural stem cells, master cells, with the ability to morph into any type of brain cell, depending on chemical signals they receive as they grow.
9. A seed planted in the ground.
10. We don't know except that it will be immortal, we will recognize one another, and we'll be like Jesus.

Chapter Five

1. John the Baptist.
2. Vapor.
3. Adam.
4. 49.24 years, 77.7.
5. Clean water, immunizations, and antibiotics.

112

6. The brain has lost all its functions, including thinking, and the control of body movement, sensation, and vital functions such as control of temperature and breathing.
7. Resurrection of the body.
8. Weakness, power.
9. My Redeemer lives, see God.
10. Changed.

Chapter Six

1. Suddenly.
2. Short.
3. Medication, anesthetics, surgery, radiation, chemotherapy, nerve blocks, cutting of nerves, relaxation techniques, biofeedback, guided imagery.
4. Different patients view "reasonable treatments" differently. The patient, if possible, should be involved in decisions about extraordinary treatments, especially those with adverse side effects.
5. No. Hospice is only palliative (comfort) care.
6. To cloak or "wrap around" a person.
7. No. Our lives are in God's hands and He numbers our days. When we ask for His will, that always leaves the window open for a miracle.
8. Generally, providing for the physical, psychological, and spiritual needs of patients.
9. Relish, accept death.
10. Just us and our Maker—our Heavenly Father who is one with our Savior.

Chapter Seven

1. The mind, will, and the emotions.
2. The Apostle Paul.
3. Reject.
4. Who am I? Why am I here? Where am I going?
5. The Lord will go with us through the valley of the shadow of death.
6. Redemption, home.
7. Elijah and Moses.
8. Witnesses.
9. The rich man who woke up in hell pleading for water.
10. At peace.

Chapter Eight

1. Child, adult.
2. Exceed.
3. We do have some knowledge because God has revealed it to us by His Spirit. Among things we know are: God will wipe away all tears, there will be no sorrow or crying, no pain or death, and there will be no night there. There will be joy and singing, recognition of people there. We will be able to eat, because there will be the Marriage Supper of the Lamb—and we'll even rule and reign with Jesus during the Millennium.
4. The Apostle Paul talked about the third heaven. Some Jews believe God's abode was in the seventh heaven. The author believes the first heaven is where clouds float and birds fly; the second heaven is where the

114 **Swallowed by LIFE**

planets and stars are located; and the third heaven is where God is and where we'll live with Him.

5. Because Jesus was seated on the right hand of the Father when Stephen died.

6. Write down your own beliefs or share with the group.

7. Believing in Jesus, that God raised Him from the dead, confessing our sins, following Him in obedience.

8. We humans like things we can see, feel, and touch. Jesus asked Philip, "Do you not believe that I am in the Father, and the Father in Me?" If we have learned to trust in Jesus, we also trust in God, because He is God the Son.

9. Because faith is necessary for salvation, because we see His handiwork, because we experience answered prayer and His work in our lives, because the Spirit bears witness with our Spirit that we are the offspring of God.

10. We're in love with Jesus.

Chapter Nine

1. Anger is one of the accepted stages of grief. Sometimes its anger turned inward, other times, anger turned outward.

2. Yes. Because God left so many testaments of His love and grace that we sometimes ignore or forget. But He is patient with us.

3. Because we sorrow not as those who have no hope. Those who move quickly to acceptance, another part of the grieving process, find peace and victory because they believe God will never leave them or forsake them.

4. Only you can answer that.
5. Swallowed, life.
6. Temporary.
7. Once, die, judgment.
8. Sins, appear the second time.
9. Hearing, reading, prayer. Why.
10. Eternal life. Swallowed.

Chapter Ten

1. A covenant, particularly between God and man. A testimony. An affirmation of beliefs or convictions.
2. Yes. You can designate who is to receive even small mementos and allow the family to know you better.
3. Feuding.
4. Avoid, death.
5. Mend broken relationships, heal hurts and misunderstandings, forgive, and love.
6. A Christian, how God impacted your life.
7. Favorite memories, funny stories, miracles and answers to prayer, things for which you thank God, thanksgiving for the person to whom you are giving the testament, a prayer for loved ones, a promise to meet them in Heaven.
8. Relate your story about testaments given to you.
9. Only you know the answer to this question, but share it with the group.
10. Give this question some thought. Then share your answer if you wish.

Made in the USA
Charleston, SC
09 December 2011